Spy in the House of Anaïs Nin

by

KIM KRIZAN

ISBN 978-1-7339922-0-6
Ebook ISBN:

Typeset by Tara Montane

Published 2019 by
Total Global Domination

Cover design by Sonia Harris

CONTENTS

INTRODUCTION

THE WRITER IS A WOMAN

CHILDHOOD AND ADOLESCENCE

EARLY ADULTHOOD AND MARRIAGE

BECOMING HERSELF

MID-LIFE COMPLICATIONS

IN THE REAL WORLD
AT LATE MIDDLE-AGE

THE FINALE

THE FUTURE

Note to the reader:

*Anaïs Nin believed one should free associate,
let fragmented images emerge, and then find
meaning afterward.*

*This collection of essays about Nin's life and writing
can be read sequentially, as presented here,
or randomly. You can, by design and at any point,
find an entrance into her world.*

INTRODUCTION

How I Came to Spy on Anaïs Nin

I had always been an exceptionally good spy. Listening covertly to whispered adult conversations, quickly rifling through the contents of a suitcase, and surreptitiously thumbing through old letters were my specialty. I could rapidly deduce complex realities – especially those of moody adults – in a flash. Poker-faced to the end, I would never reveal my knowledge, never exhibit my secrets, never betray my sources. But early in my college career I began spying on a dead woman. She was a writer of whom, until that time, I'd never heard.

What became my literary spying career started when I was an undergraduate studying literature. It was then, while browsing through a tiny bookstore in Los Angeles, I came upon the childhood diary of Anaïs Nin. I opened the book's crisp pages and read the stories of an eleven-year-old Spanish girl who had begun keeping a record of her life when she, her mother, and her younger brothers came to America by boat. These stories had begun as a simple letter to her father, a temperamental composer who had abandoned the family. Nin later said she wrote in an effort to lure him back, but her mother had discouraged her from sending the letter. Still, young Anaïs continued writing and that first missive to her father grew into a diary traversing seven decades.

I can still remember that as I stood in the aisle of the bookstore I found Nin's writing to be remarkable. Her descriptions and insights were already beyond those of an ordinary child and, though she was a product of the still-Victorian attitudes of the time, her inner journey could be wildly free and individualistic. The accompanying photographs of her wistful face underscored the loss she had endured. Reading Nin's diary made me feel as if I'd stumbled on a secret cache and was indulging in a sort of voyeurism. Though I had never heard of this writer and could not yet properly pronounce her name, I spent all my money for the week to buy her book.

I had just experienced my own traumatic loss and this may have been why her story spoke to me. My observation is this: people who are attracted to Anaïs Nin's diaries are often experiencing their own possibly violent uprootings and forced new starts. As I read through all of Nin's diaries chronologically, I found that she had survived secret deprivations and quiet desperations by breaking taboos most of us would never dare to question, with the added audacity of then revealing all in a handy set of books.

Through her writing Nin acted for me as a sort of fantasy mother, a confidante and comfort, a romantic soul who was open and free, a leading light who was reckless and glamorous. For many young people of the '60s and '70s she had been a guru untethered by societal restrictions, someone who turned the boredom and disappointments of everyday living into an extraordinary adventure tale. By the time I discovered her writing she was no longer wildly in vogue, which was fine with me for she seemed a rare treasure more suitable to privacy. Entering the world of Nin seems to open a psychic door for her readers, one that allows them to drop down an aperture and skin dive through their own feelings, dreams, and experiences.

Nin's childhood diary addicted me. And then one diary led to another, like a breadcrumb leading to another breadcrumb, clues leading to new clues and moving through the passages of her life until the end. Becoming immersed in her story, struggles, and victories created a kind of relationship between us. It was a "received" relationship, a one-way connection through time and space, one that I suppose the artist hopes for and from which the recipient benefits. And this relationship resulted in my own rejoinders. I had empathy for her. I was inspired by her. I became angry with her. I judged her. I forgave her. And 'round it would go.

My relationship with Nin via her diaries resulted in the writing of my Master's thesis, which explored the psychology of creativity. And, in an interesting turn of events, my Master's thesis led to my co-creation of the *Before Sunrise* film trilogy, the story of a young woman and man who meet on a train and have an intense, emotionally intimate connection, and then must part. It was my first film script and its sequel, in what was a shock, earned me an Academy Award nomination.

My relationship with Nin also led to letters exchanged with Nin's editor, Gunther Stuhlmann. It led to a dinner with her great love and second husband, Rupert Pole, who told me even more secrets. It led to a visit with Rupert in his and Nin's former home on a shady hillside in Los Angeles where he showed me Nin's office, as well as the final words she wrote in her final journal. My relationship with Nin also led to a trip to Louvecienne, France to see the home, then unoccupied, in which she had lived with husband Hugo Guiler and where she first met Henry Miller. And it led me to a little break-in of that home for a closer look.

As answers led to more questions about the mysteries of Nin's life, I spent hours digging through the unpublished, original materials stored at the UCLA Library. There I would enter a cool, wood-paneled room to examine the contents of Nin's files. The portions of her diary that have been published are voluminous, but the raw diary is gargantuan and I spent many happy hours making discovery after discovery. Then, as I departed UCLA at the end of the day, I would often drive east on Sunset Boulevard past the hospital where Nin died (which is now the surreally-blue Church of Scientology).

What was I searching for? I sought evidence, breadcrumbs, detritus. It was as if I was a detective following clues so as to untangle the mysteries and mythology of one life – one so complicated that Nin herself had a box of notes to keep all of her stories straight.

This research led me to consult extensively in the preparation of Nin's recently published diaries, *Mirages* and *Trapeze*. It also led to my involvement with the Nin estate, as well as my place on the board of the Anaïs Nin Foundation. And it has led to my archival work in what was Nin's and Rupert's Japanese-inspired home, which was designed by her brother-in-law Eric Wright, the grandson of Frank Lloyd Wright.

I've spent many days in the house helping Tree Wright, overseer of the Nin estate, in sifting through Nin's private possessions. I've gone through papers, manuscripts, letters, bills, and clippings. I've spied Nin's paintings, clothes, furniture, hats, mementos, souvenirs, and beauty gadgets. I've perused Nin's final medical papers and the bills from her psychologist. I've lugged out the countless manuscripts and diaries that were sent her by fans and friends, items she was loath to throw away. I've read private letters she gave to Rupert, letters that will most likely never be published. I've dangled my feet in her black pool. I've run my fingers through her indoor sand garden. I've seen her last bottle of medicine, a strong painkiller she was prescribed as she declined from cancer. I've even opened her refrigerator.

While working in the house I've talked with Nin's nephew, Devon Wright, about his frequent childhood visits with this "radiant," soft-voiced, "very different" aunt who always encouraged him and his brother to swim in her pool while she sat on the sidelines writing. I've visited Eric and Mary Wright, Nin's in-laws, and I've listened to stories of the long development of their relationships with Nin. And in working through Nin's file cabinets, I've seen the evidence of her friendships with many famous people of her time, as well as her various projects and interests. Finally, I've learned that for all the drama and secrets that swirled around Nin while she was alive, drama continues to swirl. There is intrigue behind the scenes, competition, battles.

What was the point of all this "spying"? I suppose it was to understand the material reality of someone I'd come to know so well through her writing. I am a spy in the house of Anaïs Nin, the woman who thought herself a "spy in the house of love." And, as Nin knew, our obsessions are always efforts to find aspects of our selves.

These are essays I've written about Nin, many based on research I've conducted using private materials and previously unseen documents I found while working in her home. Nin herself believed one should free oneself from linear logic by free-associating and then find the meaning afterward, much as one does when contemplating the surrealistic truths of dreams. Perhaps that's what I've done in my essays and research over these three-plus decades.

I hope you, too, enjoy "spying" on this most daring, most creative, and most visionary woman.

Nin's Life at a Glance

For those not familiar with the details of her life, Anaïs Nin was a 20th century diarist. Her first name is properly pronounced "Anna-ees." She began what became her life-long work of art in 1914 at the age of eleven and kept writing until her death 63 years later in 1977.

Nin's diary focused on her interior life and became the chronicle of her search for fulfillment in what was often for women a painfully restrictive culture.

Anaïs Nin was born in France in 1903. Her Cuban-born parents lived as genteel artists, mainly in Paris and Spain. In a blow that affected her all of her life, Nin's composer father, Joaquin Nin, abandoned his wife and children, forcing them to sail for America. While on board the ship, young Nin wrote a letter to lure him back to the family. This letter was never sent, but it was the beginning of her famous diary.

Once settled in New York City, Nin established a regular diary-writing habit, learned English, and became a voracious reader. To help her mother support the family, she dropped out of high school to become an artist's model. Still, Nin continued to struggle with sadness caused by her father's absence.

At age 20, Nin married a young banker named Hugh Guiler. They moved to Paris where she attempted to play the role of a conventional wife. Nin read contemporary literature and, though it was considered shocking for a woman to have done so, she wrote an analysis of D. H. Lawrence's controversial novels.

In 1931 Nin met the nearly destitute writer Henry Miller, as well as his wife June, and Nin and Miller had a secret affair. This began a creatively and personally fulfilling period in Nin's life, during which she associated with artists and attempted to free herself from society's confining rules. She was an early devotee of psychoanalysis and became a patient of Otto Rank, a colleague of Freud. Nin also began fictionalizing portions of her diary, which brought her some underground success. Her works included a novel titled *Winter of Artifice*; this book told the story of her dramatic reconciliation with her father.

Nin's idyllic decade ended in 1939 when, with Europe on the brink of war, she and Guiler were forced to return to New York. There she struggled to publish her highly stylized fiction while also juggling numerous relationships, including a friendship with Gore Vidal. After many frustrations in the publishing world, Nin purchased a printing press and printed her own books. Her husband contributed artwork to her books under the name Ian Hugo.

In 1947, Nin met a young man named Rupert Pole, with whom she fell in love. Unable to break with Guiler, Nin embarked on a secret relationship with Pole, all the while recording her experiences and feelings in her diary. Never a believer in laws, Nin married Pole in 1955 without divorcing Guiler. During these emotionally intense years, Nin wrote a series of "continuous novels" that fictionalized her experiences. They were ultimately published under the title *Cities of the Interior*.

While living a dual life shuttling between New York and Los Angeles during the 1960s, Nin made the risky decision to allow her diary to be published, though she chose to remove the most private details of her romantic relationships. The first installment, published in 1966, was titled *The Diary of Anaïs Nin* and it was an immediate success. Though it was a profoundly personal work, it hit a universal vein of experience – especially with women.

Nin found herself, in her sixties and seventies, playing the part of an international feminist icon.

While Nin traveled the world speaking about her writing and meeting fans, subsequent volumes of her edited diary were published. They covered the period up through the end of her life and totaled seven volumes. Finally, in 1977, Nin died of cancer in Los Angeles with Rupert Pole by her side.

Before she died, it was Nin's decision to have her early diaries published, as well as erotica she'd written in the 1940s. As a result, *Delta of Venus*, *Little Birds*, and Nin's childhood diary titled *Linotte* were released, as well as three volumes of *The Early Diary of Anaïs Nin*. Also, in a decision that generated much controversy, Rupert Pole published the "secret" or "unexpurgated" parts of her previously-released diaries. The first unexpurgated diary is titled *Henry and June*; it includes the material removed from Nin's first published diary and was made into a feature film. Other unexpurgated diaries include *Incest*, *Fire*, *Nearer the Moon*, *Mirages*, and *Trapeze*.

During her 63 years of highly personal and yet ultimately public writing, Anaïs Nin forged a style of expression that befits the 21st century. She seemed to foresee our modern era of Internet communication, even wishing for what she called a "café in space" where she could keep in touch with others. Nin believed that consciousness is a stream of images and words that flow from us as long as we live, and something to be shared.

Anaïs Nin Foresaw Social Media

Did Anaïs Nin, a 20th century diarist, foresee social media? Did she divine the self-revelatory communications we so boldly fling into the communal ether? I believe so, and it's taken the invention of the Internet to understand her work.

Nin's goal in writing was to record her life the way she saw it – or wished it to be. Perhaps this is the drive that compels all artists: the need to give form to our experience – experience that is amorphous. We are quite literally the apparatus that shapes what we produce. And after ordering our experience, whether through a diary or some other work, we may wish to share what we've made with others.

Showing the private diary she had created all her life was a tricky undertaking for Nin, partially because she did so at a time when many denigrated journal writing as a form of narcissism inferior to the lauded novel. In those days the demarcation between one's private and public life was clear, and revealing less than a polished front in what was called "polite society" was considered unseemly. But Nin believed in the importance of the personal world and doubled down, requesting that the unpublished portions of her diary be released after she died. She wanted to tell her whole story, even though it included her sex life – an area women have long fought to control on their own terms.

The first of Nin's "unexpurgated" diaries is *Henry and June*, which revealed Nin's extramarital love affair with the writer Henry Miller. Much of their relationship was spent talking or writing letters. Their time together was an avalanche, an ocean of words. It was during this heady period that Nin discovered the joy of Parisian café life: conversing with interesting people for hours, sharing stories and ideas, enjoying emotional intimacies.

Nin's hunger to merge with others continued as she went on to chronicle behavior few of us would admit or even consider. Her second unexpurgated diary, *Incest*, described Nin's brief, consensual sexual relationship with her father, a faithless Don Juan who had abandoned her when she was a child. *Fire* disclosed her complicated relationship with psychoanalyst Otto Rank, a close colleague of Sigmund Freud. And *Nearer the Moon* detailed Nin's passionate bond with Left Bank Marxist Gonzalo Moré.

The widespread response to Nin's uncensored diaries was often a form of dismissal that included withering condemnation and hostile misunderstanding. Her revelations seemed to enflame a brigade of outraged moralists who heaped scorn upon her for daring to live by her own moral code, write about her adventures, and then allow that writing to be published for all to read. We in our era might describe some of the things that were written about Nin as "slut-shaming." The result was that, in spite of the sexual revolution and the women's movement, publication of Nin's diaries ceased for a period. Nin had simply revealed too much too soon to a world that wasn't ready to hear it.

When *Mirages: The Unexpurgated Diary of Anaïs Nin, 1939–1947* was finally published, it was the first new installment of her diary in a decade and a half. Being significantly involved in its preparation, I knew it to be particularly explosive. This diary opens at the dawn of World War II when Nin fled Paris with her husband. The 1930s had been an idyllic period in her life and, for the second time, she was violently uprooted and transplanted in New York. She then began a perilous eight-year search for happiness. During this time Nin explored surrealistic writing and psychoanalysis, and also befriended or had affairs with such characters as Gore Vidal, filmmaker Maya Deren, and literary critic Edmund Wilson.

Nin's next published unexpurgated diary was *Trapeze*, the preparation of which I was also involved, and this diary tells the incredible story of Nin's secret bigamy. It is my contention that Nin created a complicated arrangement partially in an effort to free herself from what has been society's narrow, sometimes suffocating prescribed role for women with all of its confounding mixed messages.

We are now denizens of the 21st century and we stand in the blast of information gushing from the firehose that is the Internet. We realize at last that we have the right to tell our own stories in our own words and images. Who knows what our point is or what our conclusion will be, for the words and images emerge from us in a stream: a public diary of our consciousness. We seem to realize now that we cannot traffic in pure truth, but rather in our own most true version of a reality of our choosing. These are modern concepts Nin understood when she began keeping a diary at age eleven.

Before the age of social media, Nin was the high priestess of the public diary. She believed, much as we do today, that experience is something to be chronicled and shared. Her life-long diary explores mysterious areas of human life both personal and universal while also breaking the false barriers between public and private, fiction and non-fiction, diary and novel, conscious and unconscious. And she forged a style of expression that will finally find its place in this century of Internet communication, full as it is of personal confession.

Much of the world now accepts and embraces the self-expression, self-exposure, and self-analysis Nin pioneered for 63 years. It is now common for us to share our personal experiences with one another via tweeting, Facebooking, Instagramming and the like – and we become pleasantly lost in each other's journeys. Ironically, Nin wished for what she called a "café in space" in which she could keep in touch with her friends. We now participate in the café in space, but only Nin could have invented so poetic a term. And to become lost in her shimmering journey is to find the lost pieces of oneself.

Anaïs Nin has finally found her time.

THE WRITER IS A WOMAN

When I first read Anaïs Nin, I was struck by how often she referred to her gender. She seemed to find it an important distinguishing trait. Indeed, in the early 20th century the role of "lady writer" was a bit of a rarity. But Nin also had a genuine interest in women's thinking and creativity, which she saw as biologically different from male thinking and male creativity.

In the decades that have passed since Nin began writing, roles have changed and evolved, and in some ways have stayed exactly the same. The importance of the issue of "womanhood" expands, contracts, and reflects its time. One day Nin's work will be valued, not as that of a woman writer, but as a writer who happens to be a woman.

The Feminist Question

Was Anaïs Nin a feminist?

This is a question that trails her and those interested in her. Because first they said she was, and then they said she wasn't. And then they said she was again – and then they said she wasn't again.

The answer is this: to read Anaïs Nin's diaries from beginning to end is to understand her life-long struggle for freedom and fulfillment in a world that tethers us to our time, to our society, to our personality with its capacities and limitations, indeed to our biology and mortality. But we are also tethered, as Nin was, to the social and political battles of our day. And it turns out we will also be judged, whether we like it or not, according to the standards of the future.

Anaïs Nin's first published diary begins in medias res when she was a young woman living near Paris in the early 1930s. The force of her story is not the exciting new friends she'd met, including the then-unknown Henry Miller and his fascinating wife, June, but Nin's own powerful personality. In her veiled, distilled, almost allegorical style, she creates herself as a character, one who seems to have appeared fully-formed from out of nowhere.

The Diary of Anaïs Nin Volume One was published in the mid-1960s, over three decades after it had originally been written, and it was a case of auspicious timing because Nin gave the impression of having achieved in the '30s the kind of independence women of the '60s were just reaching for. As a result, the book was adopted as a manifesto by members of the burgeoning women's movement and Nin was seen as a romantic feminist Messiah. In *The Diary*'s telling, Nin has no apparent husband. No lovers are mentioned. She has no obvious source of income and seems to have no material concerns. Indeed, Nin seems the embodiment of a glamorous freedom, a total emotional liberty from the messy world.

But early on, certain facts of Nin's life started leaking out. It turned out, though she hadn't mentioned him, Nin had been married to and supported by a banker, with an incriminating emphasis on "banker." Shortly thereafter, as it was determined by women who believed their political consciousness had been enlightened, Nin wasn't a feminist after all. No, they declared, she had been too embroiled in pleasing men and therefore decidedly subjugated. Nin was seen as a muse for the likes of Henry Miller, and this made her "male-identified." Her "soft" world of feelings ("soft" being a term of derision) made her suspect. Her interest in dreams, transcendence, and beauty was outdated. But the ultimate crime, according to Nin's judges, was her reliance on her husband's income.

The catch-word of the day was "liberated," as if a woman could free herself of mortal entrapments. Total economic independence was viewed as Goal Number One. It was decided women had no need for men at all, because, as the bumper sticker said, "A woman needs a man like a fish needs a bicycle." Once discovered, Nin's silence about her husband branded her a traitor to and a failure of the women's movement. As a final insult, Nin's readers and admirers were dubbed "Ninnies."

These are the sorts of machinations that turned off many women who came of age a few decades later, making my generation reluctant to join the feminist ranks. We were sick of being bossed around, defined, judged – by men or by women. We weren't thrilled with being told what we were supposed to think and feel, or what or whom we could read. In fact, my generation sometimes found women of the "sisterhood" more dismissive and hostile than the men in our lives, which tended to negate their message of sisterhood. Perhaps our recalcitrance was evidence of their success, but we were not ready to swallow their party-line without some careful consideration.

After Nin died, her diaries were published minus the slash-and-burn editing and it was then that her edge-of-the-cliff sexual adventures were revealed. It turned out that, besides the friendship and writing camaraderie she'd so lavishly described, she had had an affair with Henry Miller. Then she had other affairs. She had undergone a grueling abortion. And let's just say things got complicated when she reunited with her father. Some readers felt betrayed by these facts of Nin's life and it became even more chic for critics to deride her. Nin's image – like one seen in a funhouse mirror – metamorphosed from inspiring to downright sick. She was roundly attacked in an article titled "Adventures of a Superfluous Woman," which was written by a woman. She was decimated in an inaccurate *New Yorker* article titled "Sex, Lies, and Thirty-five Thousand Pages," again, written by a woman. And Nin was betrayed by her friend Gore Vidal in his book *Palimpsest: A Memoir.*

The irony is, long before the women's movement of the 1960s, Nin herself came to realize her life was controlled by men. Indeed, she had spent decades exploring solutions to this all-permeating problem and she did this without a sisterhood or a movement, a magazine or a label, or even a friend with whom to discuss it. It was for most of Nin's life, as Betty Friedan described in *The Feminine Mystique,* "the problem that [had] no name." Still, Nin attempted to solve it and she kept a detailed record of that struggle in her diary.

Some of Nin's readers and critics were guilty of imposing upon her a value system that, when she was writing the bulk of her diary, had not yet been created. Lost in the mists of feminist projection was the fact Nin was born into a world still under the influence of Victorianism. Lost was the fact Nin wrote her diary when there was scant expectation women could take real control of their own lives or stories – or should want to. Lost was the fact that Nin, who had left school at sixteen to help support her family, had few opportunities for gainful employment. Lost was the rather crucial detail that Nin married a young banker at age 20, partially to save her family. And lost was the terrible truth – the inescapable fact – Nin lived at a time when women very rarely enjoyed authority or independence on their own terms.

Nin's diary quickly became a screen onto which we project our evolving perceptions. Her work became a Rorschach inkblot test onto which we reveal our own unconscious, a "Rashomon" in which different characters recount differing versions of the same event, a palimpsest on which we rewrite our changing story. And Nin was misunderstood by the feminists who had originally cast her in the role of firebrand. They had hoped her diary was a set of marching orders, instead of seeing it for what it was. As Marilyn Monroe said shortly before she died, "You're always running into people's unconscious," and our perceptions of Anaïs Nin change according to a continual re-focusing of our lens, our view of things, our unconscious needs.

In reality, as a female born into a Catholic family at the turn of the last century, Nin made a number of dramatically independent moves. In her teens, she stepped away from the Church. In her twenties, she questioned Puritanical sexual restraints and decided to have sex with whomever she pleased. In her thirties, Nin "rebelled" (one of her favorite words) against societal taboos. In her forties she graduated to flaunting the laws of the land. Finally, nearing age 50, Nin declared in her diary, "I am tired of the entire relationship to men." But instead of blaming what we would call the patriarchy, Nin did something characteristic of her, which was to take full responsibility, writing, "I give the man the reins and then feel trapped in his patterns." It dawned on Nin that in spite of all her efforts to be free, her painful dependence on men (as well as her attempts to make them dependent on her) boiled down to exactly the sort of banal detail she would later excise from her published diary:

> I am terribly tired of the enormous price one pays for protection. I should have started to build up my independence long ago. I revolted against my mother turning me into a kitchen maid and went to work. When I married, I should have worked so that Hugo would not try to enslave me to the bank. The status of a wife is worth nothing. If I had worked, I would be free and not afraid to stand alone, as I am today, for Hugo's attitude towards money is medieval.

Nin's use of the word "protection" is most interesting, because our modern word would be "support." Both have fascinating connotations, Nin's of being shielded, guarded, and defended, while our contemporary term infers that the one "supported" is propped up and given additional strength and freedom. Nin's term implies vulnerability and it is certainly true that, in the world Nin was born into, women were vulnerable. Nin had experienced first-hand the powerlessness of her mother who, once abandoned by Nin's father, had no legal recourse. After Nin married, her mother was reliant on Nin's husband's income. Later, Nin's mother lived with Nin's brother.

But if granting monetary support or protection became a currency for power, Nin attempted to turn the tables and become the one with the power. Over and over, she was attracted to men who needed her money and seemed to have no qualms in taking it. Nin very literally supported and protected Henry Miller, setting him up in a flat, giving him food and wine, and even giving him her typewriter so he could write his novel. Would-be revolutionary Gonzalo Moré, another of Nin's lovers, relied on her generous monetary gifts for many years. She even attempted to give Moré a means to earn a living by creating a printing business. Later, when Nin was involved with both her husband and Rupert Pole, Nin would take the money her husband had given her and hand it over to Pole to control; Pole then doled it back to her, questioning her every purchase.

Nin was painfully aware of the absurdity of these transactions and wrote about them obsessively in her diary. She had believed freeing herself would be accomplished by throwing off Puritanical sexual restraints, but, in the end, her sexual freedoms had only enslaved her to multiple men. Finally, Nin came to a painful conclusion: "I cannot reach a mature control of my own life." She asked herself plaintively, "Will I ever be free?"

Interestingly, Nin had found much that was positive from the men in her life and she did not view them as enemies. Hugo had given her the safety, adoration, and devotion her faithless father never granted her. Henry Miller had introduced her to sexual satisfaction, while also cheering on her writing. Gonzalo Moré had given her back her Spanish sensuality, something she felt was lost when she was uprooted to America. Gore Vidal gave her brilliant discourse and professional connections. Rupert Pole gave her a fulfilling lifetime passion. Still, in spite of constructive and satisfying experiences with men, by the 1950s Nin's intensive efforts to make a living as a novelist and build a life of her own had – in her own word – "failed." And this realization was enough to crush her.

Nin believed the only thing that saved her sanity was her diary. Within its garden walls she could see her life through a lens of her own making, and then bend and craft that life into a beautiful story. This is the essence of art. Nin wrote, "I have only been able to bear the cruelties of human life by transfigurations: art, poetry, fantasy." Then, when her diary was about to be published, Nin did what writers do, which is to edit. And this is what we all do when we try to create meaning in our lives, because, ultimately, meaning – that is, our creation of it – is not reality but, rather, our construct.

In Nin's case, she edited out a husband, she edited out his money, and she edited out her affairs. In short, Nin edited out of her story that which she wouldn't or couldn't yet explain, even to her self. And herein lay the trouble for feminists, because, by the 1960s and '70s, they saw the world through a very particular perspective and they needed – or, more accurately, demanded – Nin bend the story of her life to that perspective.

It would have been constructive if Nin's feminist critics could have had a conversation with Nin about her awakening struggle to find "liberation" – and then really listened. Nin had lived through the first half of the 20th century and could've offered a first-hand perspective many members of the women's movement simply did not have. Nin and her critics would ultimately have found much to agree upon, because while feminists would have no doubt been fascinated and heartened by Nin's solitary struggle against the problem that had "no name," many interesting issues could have been discussed: Why had Nin believed the primary issue was sexual freedom? Why did it take her so long to accept the virtues of economic freedom? Why had she fallen so easily into caretaking and championing men? Had throwing off societal taboos been more destructive than constructive? When she finally became economically independent with the success of her diary, did she find the freedom she expected? Did she come to believe "liberation" is possible? And if liberation is possible, what does it look like?

Ironically, a generation that came a few decades later, my generation, judged Nin's judges for what we perceived as their blindness and failures. My generation didn't like what we felt was the literalness and the ugly conclusions of many of those in the women's movement. We couldn't abide what appeared to be the lack of joy. We didn't understand why things we sincerely enjoyed had to be symbols of subjugation. We didn't agree that men and women had about as much in common as fish and bicycles, and, by the way, which one were we? We liked men – some of them, at least. And while we liked being able to have wide-ranging opportunities, we also liked having our dreams and indulging a craving for beauty, which is where Anaïs Nin came in.

But the truth is, in the material world, we women are still engaged in a very real battle – and so is Anaïs Nin. This is because even a private diary written by a woman about her innermost life becomes, ironically, man's property. Nin was and is controlled by men and her final efforts to get out from under their dictatorial thumbs illustrate her life-long private battle, as well as ours. Just as it is now being exposed how obscenely commonplace it is for some men in the workplace to abuse and harass female colleagues, Nin's diary – her actual voice – has been commandeered by men with the familiar air of ownership.

Take, for example, the case of Nin's editors, publishers, and representatives – some very good, some questionable and even unqualified, but almost all male. Nin's first publisher was Alan Swallow, by all accounts a brave iconoclast who saw the value of a woman's private diary and then nurtured it into a public success. But Nin was required to work with an editor, Gunther Stuhlmann. My first clue that there had been a struggle was when, while researching my Master's thesis, I visited Nin's home and had dinner with Rupert Pole. Nin had been dead for years and Pole was the keeper of the flame, centering his life on promoting his beloved's writing. It was while sitting on Nin's purple couch, Pole told me the story of what had been her increasing frustration with Stuhlmann's editing of her diary. Pole said he once came home to find Nin crying at their kitchen table because, in reviewing Stuhlmann's edits, she found he had removed the word "love" from one of her journal entries and thereby masculinized her meaning. According to Pole, tears flowed down Nin's face as she asked, "Why remove 'love'?" Indeed, why?

Years later, after Pole had died, I was doing archival work in Nin's home, studying the content of file cabinets and boxes. There, I read letters in which Nin tried to get out from under what she felt was the control of Stuhlmann. She told her representatives he was becoming "increasingly autocratic." Finally, she sent Stuhlmann a letter saying she was grateful for his hard work but would thereafter do the editing herself while allowing him to retain the title.

In another act of self-assertion, Nin had been scheduled to give a talk at a public event along with a male psychologist who taught a structured method of journal writing. Before the event took place, the psychologist got word to Nin he wanted her to try his techniques. Her response was swift: no, she would not try his techniques. "We are dealing with a male ego here," she said. Later, while on stage with the man, he became agitated because Nin attracted most of the attention of the audience. Why, she had asked the event organizer, should she do things this man's way? Why should she be a mere example of his methods? She made it clear she had her own way.

But another hurdle for Nin, another roadblock, came from women because, paradoxically, it's been nigh impossible for many of us to get past Nin's sex life. Let's face it: judgments, shaming, and public efforts to minimize and humiliate are ladled out by both men and women. Even Nancy Friday, a feminist who specialized in examining women's sexual fantasies, infamously said that Monica Lewinsky could "rent out her mouth" – truly one of the more disgusting things uttered in public about a woman. So what are readers to make of a woman who detailed decades of affairs, bigamy, even incest in her private diary – and then had the diary published? Clearly, female empowerment is not a simple matter of women freeing themselves from men. Female empowerment is a matter of freeing oneself from a prison that is constructed in the mind, then coagulates into unwritten rules of the social group, then is solidified in customs and traditions, and is finally canonized in actual law, only to travel back into the mind and emotions where all of the illogic is obscured and erased, but accepted and obeyed. Perhaps this is why Nin sought freedom on the inside, within herself.

Anaïs Nin's diary, and really all art, is best appreciated if it stands on its own and not as part of movements or agendas or politics, because then its real value can be understood. And her story can most certainly be seen as feminist – but only if its readers avoid the rather male-identified habit of parsing details while failing to see the larger picture. Nin's strength was that, instead of searching outside to see what the men who'd come before her had done, she looked inside herself to discover a new way. So, it must be asked, were Nin's feminist critics inadvertently and unconsciously disavowing her work because of their unconscious subjection to patriarchal tradition?

We are now many decades down the calendar from the original publication of Nin's diary. We are a century past its maiden voyage, when it was launched by an eleven-year-old because she was unhappy with her place in this world. The enemy Nin fought has now been given a name and women all over the world are enjoying new opportunities – and also fighting new battles. Are we more enlightened than Nin or her feminist critics had been? Or are we still beholden to the beliefs of our time, beliefs born of ancient ideas scarcely remembered, ancient ideas that gave birth to our beliefs, our culture, our sense of meaning?

In 1937, Nin described in the second volume of her diary the deep friendship she enjoyed with Henry Miller, writer Lawrence Durrell, and Durrell's wife Nancy. Long, intense discussions were their activity of choice and Nin said they would "nourish" and "stimulate" one another, but also that Miller and Durrell often "ally themselves against me." She went on to write, "My feeling for woman's inarticulateness is reawakened by Nancy's stutterings and stumblings, and her loyalty to me as the one who does not betray woman but seeks to speak for her." She goes on to describe a painfully familiar scene:

> "Shut up," says Larry to Nancy. She looks at me strangely, as if expecting me to defend her. Nancy, I won't shut up. I have a great deal to say, for June, for you, for other women.

We are all waging a battle for freedom and fulfillment and power, and Nin tried to find her own way. She did some things very differently from that expected of a woman living during her era. And then she kept a written record of those experiences, eventually sharing them with the world, to the world's delight and displeasure.

Words morph and change meaning and then reverse completely. But for now: yes, of course. Anaïs Nin was a feminist.

Observation on the Life of the Housewife

In *Volume Four* of *The Early Diary,* Nin described her life as a 24-year-old woman who had been married for four years, and she made this extraordinary observation:

August 29. [1927] ... I saw again the lady I had liked so much two years ago – but how changed! Submerged and embittered by housekeeping, the care of three children, servant problems. I have known three cases of "steady" home women going to pieces, for no apparent reason. It isn't moodiness, temperament, or anything like that. I can only explain it by a sudden sense of emptiness in their lives, or of suffocation. A regular life, such as they lead, housekeeping, canning fruit, sewing, gardening, nursing children, would drive me into an insane asylum. It makes these women irritable and restless. They have made such a frowning god of low occupations; they have let these duties rule them and dry them up, and then they expect sympathy from their husbands, gratitude from their children, love in return for the sacrifice of themselves, but how shocked they would be if they discovered that they don't deserve a bit of it. Canned fruit doesn't mean as much to a man as a living, joyful face. Some women manage to can fruit and keep their bodies beautiful and their minds awake, but as most of them can't, they ought to give up the canning.

The Diary as a Woman's Medium

This is an excerpt from my Master's thesis, titled Anaïs Nin and the Psychology of Creativity, *which was submitted in 1991. I believe that in the ensuing decades, with the advent of the Internet, the predictions made here have become a reality.*

There is very little writing by women included in the literary canon. Though until this [20th] century women were discouraged from attempting to contribute to it, the one medium sanctioned for their use was the diary.

In keeping diaries and journals, women were free to describe and reflect what has been their domain: the personal world of emotions and relationships, a world that has been assumed to be less important than that of public life. Diary writing allowed women permission to focus on themselves and thereby develop self-worth, because in writing they assumed their story was worth documenting. Nin's diary writing not only told her story, but it was also a vital means to pleasure and fulfillment in what began as a troubled life.

Ironically, because it preserves continuity and reflects the linear nature of our lives, diary writing is automatically more objective than fiction. Fiction is bound by artificial, determined limits, and is generally written after reflection and with a thematic goal in mind. Diary writing is more immediate, usually goes unanalyzed, and is truer to experience. As Nin stated in her essay "Notes on Feminism," diary writing is "not so much a mode of literature as literature is a mode of it."

As diaries become recognized as significant contributions

to the canon, women's place in literature will be secured and their struggle to find and express their voices will be dignified.

CHILDHOOD AND ADOLESCENCE

This section includes essays that analyze Nin's earliest responses to a difficult start in life.

We are all fatally formed by our childhoods, for better and for worse, and Nin began her lifelong work at age eleven after having been wounded by personal tragedy. That heartbreak implanted within her a need to create a way to insulate herself from pain, much like an oyster forms a pearl around the injurious grain of sand and, in doing so, builds a valuable gem.

Creating a New Reality

In 1914, when Nin was eleven years old, she sailed from Spain to New York with her mother and two brothers. It was at this point of transition and trauma she began writing letters to her father that were intended to lure him back to the family he had abandoned.

Nin's childhood letters, eventually published in *Linotte: The Early Diary of Anaïs Nin*, calculatedly distorted the truth so as to make the option of her father's moving to and living in America as attractive as possible. This can easily be seen from an early entry he was meant to read that recorded Nin's doctored impressions of New York City:

> August 12 [1914]. Yesterday we reached New York. ... New York is big, with buildings 20, 19 or 17 stories on each side of the street. These are office buildings. Godmother explained that since land is very expensive, they build the buildings very tall to make the most of it. ... We went down steps and afterward went on a stair case that goes down all by itself, what fun. Finally we reached home. It is a very beautiful house. ... In the morning I got up, had a lovely bath, and at 9:30 we had a delicious breakfast. ... Then I dressed and took the train to Kew. It is beautiful! In the country, pretty houses with little gardens, flowers, small neat white streets. ... Maman sings, I admire everything, I think to myself that I am in a foreign land.

Compare this with Nin's original, unedited diary entry, which had been recorded the previous day, August 11, 1914. She had removed this raw reaction from the diary, but preserved it:

The sea is gray and heavy. How different from the beautiful sea of Spain! I was anxious to arrive, but I was sad. I felt a chill around my heart and I was seeing things all wrong. ... Huge buildings in advance because they hid what I love most – flowers, birds, fields, liberty. Maman came up to me and took me for a walk, whispering in my ear the wonderful things that I was going to see. But although I admire New York for its progress, I hate it. I find it superficial. I saw it as an ugly prison. ... My head felt heavy, my heart seemed full enough to burst, I felt sad and unhappy. I envy those who never leave their native land. I wanted to cry my eyes out. ... Before going to bed, I resigned myself to not feeling sad about New York, to keep still and keep my thoughts against this country to myself. Only I am indiscreet and I have told my diary everything. You won't say anything, will you, if I tell you that I hate New York and that I find it too big, too superficial, everything goes too fast. It is just hell.

The contrast between the two entries reveals much about Nin at the age of eleven. She was intensely private and benignly manipulative, but also inclined to create a dream world so as to avoid the pain of reality. Such dedication to fantasy is difficult to maintain, yet there are some people for whom "ventures into the world of imagination are not beset with dangers ...."*

While Nin's "ventures into the world of imagination" felt vastly preferable to her reality, it is notable that the writing in the "doctored" entry is stilted and juvenile, while the original, truthful diary entry flows expressively, seemingly far beyond the level of an eleven-year-old. But Nin saw no value in these unhappy thoughts; instead, she was embarrassed by them.

---

* Field, Joanna. *On Not Being Able to Paint*. Los Angeles: J. P. Tarcher, 1957.

Nin believed her diary was a receptacle for her "real" life. She believed it was the safe place in which she retained her sanity by expressing her "truest self." In reality, Nin's diary is evidence of her need for illusion. Within it she could feel significant, filter experience, and create a life in which she was in control. Isn't this what we all do, through one means or another, to avoid pain and create meaning for our lives?

What to Wear to a
Childhood Abandonment

"When I was little, I heard Papa say that I was ugly and
the idea never left me."

— Anaïs Nin, age seventeen

There is a photo of Anaïs Nin taken at a party in the mid-
1950s in which she, at age 53, is naked from the waist up
and wearing a birdcage on her head. A decade later this
still-beautiful senior citizen donned designer miniskirts
and go-go boots. And a few years after that, while
returning to Paris to promote the writing she'd begun
there decades before, she was photographed gliding along
the streets dressed in a flowing black cape.

What can we make of Anaïs Nin's adventurous and
eccentric use of clothing? Was this habit merely a
charming symptom of her creativity? An examination of
Nin's earliest writing reveals something interesting: Nin's
stunning attire was her reaction to and protection against
a painful emotional wound she suffered at an early age.

Nin began her childhood diary, titled *Linotte: The Early
Diary of Anaïs Nin 1914–1920*, as a series of letters to her
father, a glamorous minor composer who had abandoned
the family for one of his rich, young music students. It was
then that eleven-year-old Nin, her mother, and brothers
sailed away from him and toward a new life in America.
While on board the ship she propitiously began the writing
that served as an "anchor" and "harbor" for her thoughts.

Nin's childhood diary reveals the origins of lifelong
themes, interests, and obsessions that lasted throughout
seven decades of writing. These include her central struggle
to overcome the shattering departure of her father, but also,

significantly, they detail her intense interest in clothing. Wearing beautiful clothes not only safeguarded Nin's fragile self-esteem, but her creation of an extraordinary appearance also captured the attention of others – attention that was a rebuke to her father's disinterest.

* * *

"Today I almost finished my scarf ...." This is the first mention Nin makes of clothing in one of her first diary entries, recorded in August 1914 while on the ship heading for America. Soon the family arrives in New York and young Nin is disheartened when she realizes their new life will be one of shabbiness and struggle. Immediately, the eleven-year-old begins using fantasy to transform her reality into something palatable. With remarkable insight, Nin realizes she has discovered a method for coping and she advises her diary: "Close your eyes to ugly things." She, at this young age, consciously and pointedly chooses to give her life over to "dreams."

Many years later, Nin reported that when she began her diary she made the decision to view her life as a wonderful adventure tale. Moreover, if her life was to become an exciting story, a romantic drama, then she would have to be a great actor. And what is one of the most effective means for actors to communicate their characters but through distinctive costumes?

Still, before young Nin plunged headlong into dreams and delusions, she expressed concern about her intention to disengage from reality. She asked herself whether she was

> ... becoming vain and frivolous? Am I full of the wish to be admired? ... I am a little bird, I say, who has neither the strength nor energy, no nest, no place where I can lean and learn to be reasonable.

As the diary reveals, she continues to fly to "dreams," searching for the means to be happy, and many of Nin's first expressions of joy describe her clothes. She writes: "I am delighted! Godmother just made me a present of a pretty red flannel kimono. It's so warm, so soft!" Two pages later she records a gift of "4 pairs of long black stockings and one yellow pair." And after a lecture on the life of Marie Antoinette to benefit the children of Brittany, Nin creates a detailed description of the costumes worn by a model during the lecture.

Shortly thereafter, Nin's "Maman" begins what seems an enabling campaign, one apparently intending to give Nin the happy girlhood that had been compromised by her father. Thus, on a Friday in February 1915, Nin writes:

> Maman went out with me by myself and bought me some beautiful black shoes with rubber soles to keep me from the damp. I was very pleased and kept looking at them, but Maman hadn't finished. She also bought me a pretty dress in navy-blue serge with light-blue trimming at the neck and a smart white collar.

Nin continues faithfully recording each acquisition: "I received a pretty white jacket from Godmother and a hat for school. Maman is going to buy me another one for dressing up." These purchases were significant, because Nin wrote much later of feeling intense shame on her first day of school in America. Not only could she not yet speak English, but as she was introduced to the students she wore a shabby dress and would remember the feeling of humiliation all of her life. For this reason, the arrival of a package from rich relatives was exciting and noteworthy: "Maman received a trunk full of clothing from Cuba. I received a beautiful pair of shoes and a jar of 'guava cream,' a specialty of Havana."

Three months later, less than one year after the family's

arrival in America, Nin has clearly begun transmuting the pain from the loss of her father into a love of clothes:

> Two years, two years since Papa left me at Arcachon. A terrible betrayal seized me that day, I have never felt the pain of separation so deeply. Ah, poor Papa, when will you come, when shall I be able to kiss you and carry out my filial duties toward you? The other day I had a visit from a gentleman who is an uncle of one of Papa's pupils; he brought two packages from Papa. What a nice surprise! As soon as he left I opened the first package, a box camera with films for Thorvald, a gold stickpin for Joaquinito and a pretty leather purse with my initials on it for me. I was mad with joy. Dear little Papa, how nice you are! Yesterday Maman bought me a beautiful blue ribbon for my hair and a pair of white shoes. I am so spoiled.

Clothes have become an oasis of pleasure, a substitution for the love of an absent parent.

But in her lingering sorrow, young Nin finds yet another way to distract herself. In November 1915, when she is twelve, she daydreams of a boy and this "calms [her] pain." It is the first mention in her diary of what was to grow into the obsession for which she became famous. In the meantime, the detailed descriptions of clothing continue. On Christmas 1915 Nin receives "a paint box and an embroidered collar and cuff set from my aunt, and Maman had given me, the day before, a scarf and a pink cotton bonnet." She reports that on April 29, 1916 she and her mother "went to Franklin Simon and Lord & Taylor where Maman bought me shoes, stockings, ribbons and some other things." And then, Nin prepares for a special day in June when she will appear as a dancer in a performance about Joan of Arc at the Union Square Theatre. For this occasion, Nin's mother buys her "beautiful patent-leather shoes and silk stockings and gloves." With the arrival of the big day, Nin writes that she had felt disgusted by the performance hall with its odors and atmosphere of "the worst kind who act in vaudeville," so she focuses on her costume:

> ... a little white blouse, a long dark-green skirt with a little black velvet ribbon near the hem, and a black velvet bodice that laced in front. A little black apron made me look like a peasant from Lorraine, which was how I was supposed to look. I let my hair down and put on a white bonnet with a little black ribbon. ... [At] one moment I dared to raise my eyes and where the audience was I saw ... a big black hole and just a few faces. That's all. The second time, I was braver and I looked: I saw hands applauding. When we left the stage ... that vague sound of applause haunted me for a long time. It wasn't for me, it was for all of us, and yet a voice whispered, "You would like that applause for yourself." ... Dearest Diary, isn't that one more sign which should convince me that my vocation is to seek applause? I think so, and I begin to dream again.

Beautiful clothing and positive attention have married in the fourteen-year-old Nin's mind. The pursuit of such pleasures has become a means for easing her loss.

Yet, in spite of these dreams and triumphs, Nin is not a happy girl. A photo of her from around this period reveals an adolescent with long dark hair who wears a black double-breasted coat and knitted stocking cap. What is notable is her serious, even morose, expression. But once again, Nin demonstrates she is conscious of her choice to immerse herself in fantasy:

> If by romantic they mean someone who dreams, I am a romantic, but I shall keep it a secret and never dream except with my diary. ... Let's quickly take off our crown

of dreams, our coat of "what I believe" and put on the dirty apron of "what is happening."

And so Nin continues focusing on what she believes, describing what she wore on her sixteenth birthday:

A pretty light-blue dress, the shoulders covered with a big piece of blue tulle that made a charming effect. I wore silk stockings and narrow little shoes, also a coral necklace that Maman had given me for the occasion, and my hair was pulled back in a chignon of curls with a narrow blue ribbon around my head. As guests, we had my friends from school and, for the first time, a few young men. Among other things, we pretended to know how to dance and the rest of the party turned into a real dance. I was delighted and I danced a lot. I was spoiled, I received a large number of gifts and compliments.

Around this time, young Nin also seems to become conscious of the wider world of fashion and the effect it has on the opposite sex. While walking along Broadway with her friend Frances, she observes the scene:

I can't describe the men, who were of all ages and dressed every possible way, but the women! Heavens! ... We saw all those ladies walking with little tiny steps. They almost all looked like painted dolls. Each was surrounded by several men and they looked terribly artificial. The more extravagantly they were dressed, the more attention they got from the opposite sex, which would stop walking to admire them.

In the sixteen-year-old's mind, beautiful clothes, particularly extravagant clothes, have become the catalyst for attention from men.

For adolescent Nin, clothes also became the occasion. On April 9, 1919, she writes: "Maman took me downtown and bought me a pretty serge cape, patent-leather shoes, black silk stockings and gloves, and we came home very happy." Two days later, she records: "I wore my cape and my beautiful new shoes for the first time, which meant that I went to my dancing lesson putting on more airs than usual." On April 18, she writes:

> ... the weather was beautiful today and I took pleasure in letting my cape float in the breeze. It's a feeling that always makes me think of poets. And a cape can make you believe that you are someone powerful like Napoleon, or a queen with a cloak of diamonds and rubies, or just a girl dressed "in the fashion of France" (as the song says).

Soon after she takes another walk, specifically to see Easter hats: "In the street, all the ladies have new hats, pretty straw hats with flowers, like mine." And finally, because she is going on a horseback riding date with friends, young Nin reveals her main concern to be the clothes she will wear as she describes the rental of her boots and the fact that her mother and aunt help her dress:

> First I put on a linen blouse with a big collar and a black ribbon tied in a bow, then a jacket of light gray "crash," almost white. A pretty little cane completed my disguise. ... Maman was tying my hair into a bun and putting powder on my face at the same time. But when I was ready, a murmur of admiration ran through the entire family .... A horseback ride is like a trip to fairyland ....

What goes unmentioned in her diary entry is the fact, revealed years later, that during the ride a pin stuck into her flesh, yet the very real sting of the pin was erased from her romantic tale.

Nin was amazingly cognizant of wresting her pain into a desire for admiration and she begins to worry:

> One thing weighed heavily on me: I have been very pleased about receiving compliments. But the good priest

laughed heartily, and told me it was nothing at all. On the contrary, he added, it's quite natural.

She observes that she seems to have two faces, two personalities – and one is that of her practical, sociable mother, while the other is of her "philosopher" father. She writes:

> When I left home, I was powdered, painted and curled, and in the mirror I saw Maman's image. When I came back, I was pale, serious, pensive and tired, and my hair was disarranged, and in the mirror I saw Papa's image.

It becomes obvious that underneath Nin's obsessions and fantasies is an original wound, a wound even greater than the one caused by the separation from her father. In spite of the pretty dresses and admiration, young Nin begins to approach her primal insecurity, saying, "But more than ever, when I look at myself in the mirror, I think I look sad because I am not pretty, and sometimes I would really like to be pretty." And so she returns to her preoccupation with clothes:

> It's this evening that I am going to Emilia's and even if it's only one o'clock and we aren't going until 8:30, being a Nin I can't help getting ready well ahead of time. That's why my pink checked gingham dress is swinging on a hanger, my patent-leather shoes are set out next to my pair of black silk stockings, my white gloves are washed, my handkerchief is perfumed (already) and I have in front of me a little pink hat, very soft and very pretty, that Maman bought me a few days ago.

Nin's interest in dress is encouraged and supported by her indulgent mother. Nin describes more purchases:

> A pink ball gown with a great deal of tulle and a big rose at the waist, a navy-blue taffeta dress with funnel- or

bell-shaped sleeves, an adorable black velvet jacket, two blouses, one made of georgette and the other of pink net, a pink silk skirt to go with the blouses and the jacket, silk stockings, and – I think that's all ... [For] those unaccountable frivolities for a spoiled girl, Maman spent the fabulous sum of $113.75. An amazing thing! she has no regrets at all.

The "fabulous sum," circa 1919, would be the equivalent of over $1600 today, a steep bill for a single mother struggling to support three children. Nin then goes on to describe more ways her mother has coddled her, explaining that while she has new silk stockings, everyone else in the family wears old stockings that have holes. Why Nin's "Maman" singles her out for special luxuries is not mentioned, but Nin believes herself to be "extravagant." She writes of an outing: "I was very glad to go to the cinema, if only because I could wear my little velvet hat embroidered with a red rose and my black jacket, which made a stunning outfit. That shows how extravagant I am."

Young Nin, whose life at this point seems mainly housework, diary-writing, and fantasy, begins relating strongly to her absent father:

Once I put on a floppy black bow tie, which is one of the things I love enthusiastically, and Maman told me that Papa never wore anything else – always a floppy black bow tie. That seemed such an amusing discovery, and such a plausible reason for the liking I have for a black bow, that I was delighted. The whole world can make fun of me ..., but if Papa could wear a big floppy black bow tie, I am proud to share his taste and do the same!!! Hurray for the artist's bow tie!

Thus, she begins to identify with her father, to embrace him by means of style.

Nin's father, a pianist and composer, was known to be attractive, fastidious, and self-indulgent. Sharing these traits seems to be a way his daughter can be close to him, and so she continues describing her beautiful attire and appearance:

> ... one of my extravagances was an adorable pink dance dress with a lot of tulle and a beautiful rose at the waist, but really as simple as it is beautiful and original. I wore it last night with silk stockings and black shoes, and a little piece of pink tulle with fringes of little white pearls, but not a single piece of jewelry because it seemed to me the rose was perfect by itself. My hair, which I fixed with Monsita's help, was artistically arranged in a chignon of curls, like the night of Emilia's concert but even better. My dress was so pretty that the whole family and the people in the house came to the room to see it and exclaim over it.

On the next page she tells her diary: "I want to give you the good news that I have finally adopted the serious chignon as my coiffure." And then nine pages later she confesses to another exorbitant shopping spree hosted by her mother:

> If you like, I will frighten you with the price of my new ensemble. Look:
>
> | | |
> |---|---|
> | 1 Ermine | $40 |
> | 1 Velvet Dress | 29.50 |
> | 1 coat | 49.50 |
> | | $119.00 |

At the heart of Nin's fascination with style is a feeling of being closed out, barred from the celebration of life. In October of 1919, she stands in her house and watches people enjoying an elegant party across the street. Interestingly, instead of describing their appearance, she records her own. She is standing, she writes, "in my nightgown and blue slippers, with my hair hanging down and the brush in my hand." She demonstrates an extraordinary awareness of self and continues pointedly making herself the central character in her story, with an emphasis on costume.

Perhaps inevitably, Nin's family experiences a crash in their finances and her mother is worried. Still, Nin finds another way to pursue what has now become an agenda, for she can create her all-important costumes with her own hands. In late November of 1919 she writes:

> I have discovered that I can make hats. Last Saturday I took a little black tulle from an old ball gown of Maman's, the helmet of an old hat of Aunt Antolina's, and a blue flower, and I made a hat that I wore to go to Mass. To my great surprise, first Maman, then Aunt Antolina, Aunt Lolita, the neighbors, etc. etc., all told me that it was very pretty and added that they would like to know where I bought it.

After five years, Nin has gained enough confidence to try to woo her father. In a letter to him, she writes: "I already wear my hair in a bun, because I feel so serious. ... I should be a lady painter because I was born to wear a black velvet coat and the artist's floppy bow tie." But instead of luring her father to America, Nin begins to get attention from American boys. While sledding with friends, a group of young men call her "White Cap" because of her white beret, and invite her to ride with them. The girls who are present seem jealous and Nin overhears one refer to her as "the biggest flirt!" It is obvious young Nin's campaign for admiration is a success.

Finally, Nin's seventeenth birthday arrives on February 21, 1920. Formal portraits are taken and Nin's mother will host a party. In more ways than one, it is Anaïs Nin's "coming out." She has transformed her loss, set the stage for a writing career, and become beautiful and charming. Pain has given her purpose. As she and her mother plan her party, Nin admits the thing that interests her most "is the dress I will wear!" Her mother selects the dress in secret and when Nin finally sees it she is thrilled. And then Nin reveals the very heart of her psychic wound, the source of all her creativity, her raison d'etre:

> Dearest diary, I am sure, I know by a million signs, that I am not ugly any more! I have left behind the period of straight hair, unruly locks, shiny nose, sallow skin – in a word, all the horrors and horrible features of a schoolgirl – all that is past. ... When I was little, I heard Papa say that I was ugly and the idea never left me. I didn't even try to see if it wasn't true until now.

Thus, on the occasion of her seventeenth birthday and after almost six years of struggle, Nin conquered her father. By means of diary writing, beautiful clothing, and earning the attentions of others, she had not only proven her father wrong, but also become worthy of him. She is a girl so lovely, so charming, so artistic, so stylish, she is like one admired in great theatrical dramas and she goes on to write: "I wore my fairytale dress, a crown of flowers on a gold ribbon, my shoes with the Louis XV heels ...."

* * *

At age eleven, after having endured the most painful blows of her life in the form of rejection and abandonment by her adored father, Anaïs Nin made her decision and recorded it in her diary. For her, life would be transformed into a magical drama and she would become its star. Her métier would be accomplished to a large degree through costume. These efforts were undertaken to bring her the attention and admiration, in short, the love she craved.

And so it would be birdcages against the ugliness, miniskirts against time, flowing capes against the ravages of a harsh reality.

EARLY ADULTHOOD AND MARRIAGE

After having been forcefully separated from her father, Nin, at the age of 20, once again found herself living with a man: her new husband, Hugh Guiler. I find this period a particularly interesting one for Nin because, instead of accepting the reality of her new marriage, young Nin tried to force it to become the fantasy of her dreams. The differential between illusions and reality eventually caused a painful split within Nin, one she struggled to breach.

The following essays examine Nin's life during the early period of her marriage and through different lenses. They detail how Nin, a fantastic homemaker and incredibly stylish woman, began in these years to amplify a life-long habit of keeping secrets from those closest to her.

Portrait of the Artist as a Homemaker

Because she viewed her homes as stages for great dramas, Anaïs Nin was a markedly fabulous homemaker.

As an idealistic newlywed living in a New York bungalow in 1924, she kept scrapbooks of ideas for interior decoration and lavished her home with attention, painting her dining room blue and her bedroom rose and gray. She even went so far as to paint her husband's hairbrushes to match the room.

When she and her husband moved to Paris and found a flat on the Left Bank, Ms. Nin decorated it in a "modernization of the Oriental style," complete with a "Moorish bed" she found in an antique shop. She hung exotic lamps, draped shawls over her furniture, and created each room as if she were setting the stage for a romantic drama. After her business-smart American husband received a raise from his appreciative Parisian employers, Anaïs filled their apartment with gothic furniture and hired a maid.

The stock market took a dramatic tumble a few years later and the couple was forced to find more modest accommodations in the Parisian suburb of Louveciennes, so they rented a crumbling 200-year-old cottage (the yard of which was said to have been the landing spot for Madame DuBarry's guillotined head). Nin immediately set to work, painting each room to inspire certain moods. She hung "yards and yards of turquoise green velvet for the studio window," affixed a mosaic of blue stones to her fireplace, and bought an elaborately beautiful aquarium of glass fish to sit on the mantle place. She described this house as bringing a world of excitement to her.

After World War II broke out and Nin was forced to flee France, she turned on a dime and created a modern New York apartment, but had her friends paint the many windows to look like a pagan cathedral of stained glass. Then when she began an alternate life on the West coast with her "other husband," they lived in a Japanese-inspired abode designed by Eric Lloyd Wright and built in a hilly area of Los Angeles that on clear days had a view of the ocean. Nin saw to it that this, her final home, was minimalistically pure, spacious, and filled with light. It had an indoor sand garden, walls decorated with avant-garde artwork, a fireplace that Nin thought looked like it belonged in a castle, and a black swimming pool surrounded by willowy trees.

Nin's second husband, Rupert Pole, claimed that after she died and her ashes were scattered in the sea, the tree that had obscured their view of the ocean inexplicably died and allowed him to see his beloved's final resting place.

Costumes for a Great Drama

All of her life people commented on Nin's extraordinary appearance, but she really hit her stride in the late 1920s and early '30s while living in Paris. Here is a partial list of Nin's "costumes" as described in *The Early Diary of Anaïs Nin, Volume Four 1927–1931*:

"Tight-fitting dark blue velvet dress with enormous medieval sleeves slit to show half the arm"

"Black velvet dress with black lace sleeves and black hat with veil over the eyes – and all my favorite Florentine jewelry"

"Gold lamé turban ... to go with my gold lamé dress"

"Hair up and slick (with water), earrings, black velvet dress, and my shawl from Granada"

"Black silk coat, coral silk dress, very tight-fitting, with a row of black buttons, and a three-cornered black hat with a veil"

"Red-and-black Grecian dress"

"A white evening dress, a red carnation, Molyneux 'Fete' perfume"

"Turquoise Grecian cape and dress and black hat ... an accroche coeur [literally, a hearthooker] on my forehead"

"Jade green cape"

"A red-and-white sheer chiffon dress without sleeves"

"An indescribable green dress made by the Russian woman according to my design, a subtle, insidious dress, revealing and concealing the figure at the same time,

Oriental in essence, complex in its embroidery, entirely unintelligible ..."

"Black turban"

"Yellow Spanish dress"

"Black underwear, my black velvet dress, coral earrings and bracelet, Egyptian perfume, my black hat and fur coat"

"Green dress and gold slippers"

"Vaporous turquoise dress and cape and hat, hair made black with water, eyelashes heavy with paint, eyelids painted green (as per the suggestion of Natasha) and, oh, very crimson lips and tinkling bracelets, and all the cheap seductions (except for perfume, because it isn't cheap enough)"

"Sky blue dress and blue linen hat ... cretonne bag and cretonne umbrella"

"Long amethyst chiffon dress and sandals"

"Beautiful Chinese pajamas from the Biarritz"

"Chinese red-and-black silk coat"

"Asiatic-Russian old rose costume, as for a Byzantine opera"

"A pair of lace gloves, a red picture hat, a little red jacket, a Robertson clan plaid skirt, a turquoise cape dyed black, several evening dresses lengthened, new petticoats made out of artificial silk"

"I have time to re-dye my black gloves with India ink. They were worn and turning white."*

---

* During this period, Nin's favorite perfume was Mitsouko by Guerlain.

The Birth of Nin's Secrets and Lies

Woe the poor secret. She is out of fashion.

We live in an age when keeping anything to ourselves is believed to be an act of dishonesty exacting a damaging emotional price. Consequently, we collectively indulge in the habit of getting it all out, which simply means blabbering everything that flits through our minds in the name of truth. And this public exposure of what were once secrets seems to have become a purifying act, one with almost ritualistic elements.

"Honesty" has extended to all manner of human experience. Our judgments and opinions are splayed over the comment sections of websites. We yell into our cellphones while standing on street corners, blurring the line between the insane and those merely talking to their spouses. Meanwhile, comedy routines performed by respected talents deal with subjects hitherto unmentioned, such as bodily functions and sexual problems. It seems all sources of embarrassment and shame are in play.

Psychologist Michael Slepian says that merely thinking about secrets makes people feel "disingenuous and inauthentic." An October 2017 article in *Psychology Today* titled "Under the Skin" by Micaela Heck claims the unhealthy impact of secrets may be caused by the way they "lurk" and "nag" at us. The article goes on to list our modern conception of "top secrets" as, in order: extra-relational thoughts, sexual behavior, ambition or plan, sexual infidelity, lying, finances, non-drug habits, sexual or gender identity, mental health issues, and belief or ideology.

The fact is, though, that much of our experience is ours privately – and therefore, by definition, secret. How can we express the most elusive of our perceptions, feelings, epiphanies? Language is a limited technology and words are merely tools, therefore we have an inadequate vocabulary with which to describe the magnitude of experience. And is this so wrong? Greta Garbo said, "There are many things in your heart you can never tell to another person. They are you, your private joys and sorrows, and you can never tell them. You cheapen yourself, the inside of yourself, when you tell them."

Still, according to Slepian, there is another option: writing. And what is diary-keeping but an effort to tell oneself the story of her (or his) life, to give experience order, to create meaning. Anaïs Nin, who began diary writing as a child and well before our Age of Purge, became in the pages of her journal a secret-confessor extraordinaire, but eventually chose to publish her private diaries. She had always believed her "truest half" resided there, so permitting its publication was an attempt to share that self with the world.

By the mid-1920s, Nin's writing habit was over a decade old. Her diary chronicled a painful departure from both her father and Europe, adjustment to America, adolescence in New York, the early years of her marriage to Hugh Guiler, and a move to Paris in December 1924 when she is 21 years old. *The Early Diary of Anaïs Nin, Volume Four 1927–1931* is the last of her early unexpurgated diaries. It covers the years immediately before she met Henry Miller, the story of which was revealed in her first published diary, *The Diary of Anaïs Nin 1931–1934*.

I feel that *The Early Diary 1927–1931* is one of Anaïs Nin's most interesting books. During her mid-twenties Nin was rapidly maturing, her character was solidifying, and during this period she describes exploring new psychological and emotional territory, as well as new behaviors. Also in this diary, without the editing or expurgating that would complicate her next published diaries, Nin begins keeping what we would think of as "top secrets."

*   *   *

At age 23, after having lived twelve years in Puritanical America, Anaïs Nin and her banker husband Hugh Guiler, as well as her mother and younger brother, moved to Paris. Though Nin had been born in France, she at first found herself resisting its lure. Gradually, though, Nin's primness began to dissolve and she acclimated to Parisian sensibilities. This was, as she described in her diary, a "brutal awakening." Nin wrote of feeling that something bad was developing within her, that something was "wrong" with her:

> ... the Devil is in me and awakening noisily. But no one can say I didn't struggle two and a half years against European tolerance, humanity (which is another way of saying weakness), against its satanic flexibility, its lack of conscience, scruples and humility.

Nin remembered that in her early days of diary writing, while still a child writing in French, her style was "franker, sharper ... until I fell into Victorianism. Can I ever make up for that blunder?" And though she is adoring of her husband, she observes what she believes is the "suffocation" and emptiness in the lives of housewives. Interestingly, this most cerebral of women believes she is moving from a life of ideas to one of sensations. She goes on:

> ... the physical is trying to regain its place. I am harder emotionally. I am wide awake, strong, intensely alive, but less idealistic, and my moments of supreme spiritual goodness have gone. ... I shall find a way of living my life without pain to others. This sudden and absolute

intellectual and physical freedom distresses and yet intoxicates me.

As the diary pages turn, Nin writes of something she describes as "hunger," but hunger for what? She enjoys the admiration of her much older Spanish dance teacher and details their relationship in her diary. It is not an extramarital affair she pursues, because when she suspects an acquaintance of having one she sternly condemns it in her journal. Still, desire, dreams, and imagination fuel her. John Erskine, an American novelist who was her husband's professor in New York, becomes an important new social contact. Nin is in awe of him and fantasizes about a friendship with him. She also develops a deep emotional connection with her cousin Eduardo. Nin realizes she gives an impression of harmless sweetness and this hides her intensity, sorrow, and loneliness. She wonders why her life as it is with a loving husband, a caring mother and brother, and engrossing dance classes is not enough. Then she remembers an epiphany, one she would recall for years to come: "Even last year, walking down Boulevard Montparnasse, I asked myself what could happen if suddenly I said and did exactly what I wanted to say and do." Finally, she admits to her diary in French, "I am not happy here."

Nin writes that she had begun her marriage at age 20 by living only for her husband. Indeed, diary entries from her early years as a bride are full of romantic descriptions of Guiler's perfection, his beautiful temperament, his "cat-like" personality. But after five years of marriage, Nin feels she is mentally living other lives and it worries her. She writes:

From the beginning I feared that he could occupy only part of me, that he is the Master of one life and no more. I am, against my will, a vagabond, a wanderer, a complex troublemaker. I must at least live without hurting him. ... I cannot stay home. I have a desperate desire to know life, and to live in order to reach maturity.

Nin struggles to articulate this quest for a Holy Grail of unknown identity, writing, "What attracts me, tempts me perpetually, is the opportunity to live out a new self ...." It seems Nin finds "a new self" – or a new aspect of herself – in every man she meets. Does this make up for the father who did not adore her, who left her feeling invisible and unlovable? Erskine, the same age as her father and, like her father, a successful artist, becomes a more frequent character in her diary and an obviously god-like presence in her mind, one who both intimidates and attracts her.

As the months pass, Nin consciously explores flirting. She realizes her dance teacher is reinvigorated because of her interest in him. Nin's exploration of Spanish dance is an important turning point in her life and in August of 1928, when she is 25 years old, she writes:

Does one come to France to learn the power, the inevitable power of the body? I have leapings of sensuousness entirely separate from myself, from my dreams, my soul, my feelings. There are moments when I do not belong to myself. Sudden desires for an unknown love, sudden curiosity about an unknown man, a sudden melting of the body into a dream, a surrender. And this does not happen in moments of idleness, but unexpectedly .... I adore, I worship Hugh with my body and soul. But I have a surplus of affection, of enthusiasm, which is pent up ....

Nin blames these frightening but delightful new feelings on her "devilish" and "demoniac" imagination.

Meanwhile, Erskine, a much older married father of two, still frightens her. As Nin and Guiler socialize with this glamorous man, she is inordinately focused on him, on how she feels with him, on how to make him interested in her, on how to dominate him. The fact that he is a famous novelist in America is a tremendous draw for her, for she likes creative men. She confides to her diary she is disinterested in Guiler's banking life. She had hoped – and still hopes – her husband will become an artist.

Nin is changing and her family notices. Guiler is concerned about some of her writing, which he says is "wild." She claims in her diary to have been an ideal wife and daughter, not only chaste and obedient, as were the values of the day, but also innocent and idealistic. She is frankly tired of this role and wants to grow – and growing she is. Her brother Joaquin confesses he doesn't like the new her. She placates him by claiming "the new her" is just a phase, but then records otherwise in her journal. She writes that she has grown up and feels hungry for life.

And then, a sea change. The recurrent sense in Nin's early diary that she is romanticizing and idealizing herself gives way to a new honesty when she divulges:

> I am only beautiful at moments, here and there, by a trick of clothes, or expression, or emotion. ... While I have my days, my face changes perpetually, with an idea, with a hat which involves the East, with the expression of my dancing. Looked at coldly, I have a small face suggestive of old paintings but not strictly classical, fine features and big eyes but teeth like a mouse's, just a hint of sauciness in the nose, and hair that is neither black nor blond. How often I have described myself but never with such cynicism. ... [When] I meet someone who is both intelligent and lovely, then I feel Hugh did not get much out of life.

She imagines writing a book with her husband as protagonist and herself as a comical and ridiculous character, culminating with the husband character leaving her.

Finally, a moment for which Nin has longed: she

becomes Erskine's confidante and he her friend. Erskine listens as she reads passages from her diary, an incredibly intimate and exciting event in her life. Much to Nin's delight, Erskine tells her he loves her clarity and style, and then goes on to confide in Guiler that he believes Nin is finding herself and her writing will "coagulate into something all her own." Nin is ecstatic. She feels she has won over her "most discerning critic," and this gives her a blast of confidence.

Nin is now actively trying to find her power in the world. As a young woman living in the early 20th century, one who was abandoned by her father, one who does not have a high school diploma but who has read and written voraciously for many years, she feels she must find her medium. Tellingly, her medium is men, for she is drawn to flirting with womanizers, seeing if she can conquer or impress them. To the discerning reader, these men are most certainly versions of her father, though she seems unaware of this obvious parallel. Nin is cognizant, though, she does not have real interest in the men, but is merely testing her flirting power.

It is at this dangerous moment Nin's diary reveals the very first criticisms of her heretofore perfect husband. She describes Guiler as "tranquil," expressing "misty appreciation," having "no opinion," being given to "passive and calm rumination." He is completely absorbed in his bank work, which frankly bores her. She believes her husband is deep and fine, but not brilliant and startling. And then Nin turns her criticisms on herself, writing that because she keeps a journal and has not produced much else except attempting a few stories, she considers herself a fake. This issue, that of the value of diary writing, continues to trouble her for many years as she searches for a way to share her work with the world.

As the diary pages turn, Nin begins to ruminate on

adultery. Extramarital affairs are not only acceptable, but also fashionable in France. The Catholic country turns a blind eye to adultery, because divorce is an unpardonable sin. Affairs have become a kind of cultural reality; it is believed wives who do not indulge in them are cold or unsophisticated. Still, Nin is inclined against adultery because she believes her writing will fulfill her overflowing feelings.

Nin and Guiler continue to grow closer to Erskine and his family, so they meet for a vacation in Dijon. This is another special moment for Nin, because Erskine tells Guiler that Nin's writing is truly good, that "she is a writer." This gives Nin a feeling of courage, one that ignites a new confidence in herself. Guiler observes she "is no longer suffering life," but beginning to "dominate" it.

And then Erskine kisses her. After this seemingly spontaneous act, Nin suffers in a state of painful confusion. The kiss becomes a precious possession, a valuable secret that lives within her. She is thrilled that the object of her great admiration has "lost his head" over her, but she is left with a feeling of discombobulation. Erskine then appears on the doorstep of her apartment when he knows Guiler is at work. Nin invites him in and they quickly tumble together in passionate kissing. Erskine asks her to show him her body. She leaves the room, then returns wearing only her Spanish shawl, willing to give all, but Erskine can't perform sexually. He explains that he feels guilty about his friend Hugo. Erskine exits, and then he and his family depart for America, leaving Nin so devastated she cries in the street. Guiler seems dimly aware. He says he feels jealous of his friend and is glad he's gone.

This incident, which Nin duly records in her diary but does not mention to a soul, is what we 21st century inhabitants would think of as her first "top secret." She is astounded at her own reaction, exclaiming, "My secret does not poison me!" But she also calls herself "a liar." Still, she writes that her lies do not matter and, for the first time, describes what will become a mainstay in her life: the "Mensonge Vital," the "vital lie," the conscious creation of an illusion that is not harmful but, rather, gives life. She writes, "Truth in itself is not worth more or is not more right than untruth, loyalty than disloyalty, sincerity than insincerity; but wisdom lies in knowing how and when to use them all." This is a dramatic psychological crossroads for Nin, because she runs the risk of emotionally isolating herself from others.

"I long ..." In craving the approval of Erskine, Nin has recreated the longing she felt for her absent father. This longing was sexualized when what she really desired was adoration, something her husband certainly does demonstrate, though his love does not quench her hunger. Nin begins to fear she resembles her womanizing, lying father in that their "deceptions" are similar. She writes that she loves her husband and that he deserves to be loved, but she needs other joys and ecstasies. She wonders, "... doesn't he miss all the sweetness other women could give him?" She also wonders what psychological problems are caused by the intense frustration she feels. Nin admits to herself she "longs," but her desires conflict with her husband's happiness.

For the first time, in the midst of her praise of Guiler's greatness and profundity, real disenchantment emerges. Nin records in her diary that her husband is amazingly misty, can barely remember his childhood, dithers over choice of food "or even a tie," wavers, is vague. She writes that only in Guiler's work is he sure and direct. But then, almost in argument with herself, she explains that he chose to marry her against his family's wishes and therefore lost his inheritance, that his family considers him a black sheep. As a result of her frustrations with her husband's lack of clarity in contrast with her own intensity, imaginative passions become her escape. Nin writes that she hopes to some day become "domesticated and quiet," though she can't stand the normal women she meets with their banal preoccupations. Nin debates with herself, writing, "Something in me curses away all peace."

In the fall of 1929, the economy collapses. Nin's 31-year-old banker husband had, until this moment, not only afforded her a comfortable life, but also expected an early retirement. Suddenly, the couple faces "the ruin of his [financial] speculations." As Guiler counts his money, Nin slowly realizes her husband had given her the leisure to build her inner world. She then faces the "sad days" of news of suicides over decimated fortunes, and she and her husband realize their savings has been lost. She writes, "All expenses to be cut short," but claims she's "glad to be deprived again – all my childhood was spent in that state ...." Nin believes she's had too many pleasures and writes, "We are going back to the simple life." She puts on a strong face for Guiler and "the world," but then turns to her journal where she shows her "real lack of mettle."

The reality of their diminished finances and the fact that they must give up their glamorous apartment seems to lead to more clarity. Nin admits in her diary, "The struggle to make something great out of myself without being egotistical is almost impossible to endure." She comes to believe her husband is limited and insufficient, and the realization she is beyond him makes her take to her bed and shiver. Nin is disappointed intellectually – the thing that is most important to her. She writes that the day of this awareness is the most unhappy of her life. But she distracts herself. She fantasizes about meeting Erskine, which makes her feel happy again.

Then Nin discovers D. H. Lawrence's novel *Women in Love*. She ruminates in her diary on the fact that Parisian women have lovers and states again that the phenomenon of the secret lover was created by the Catholic Church. Meanwhile, an older woman of 60 urges Nin to take one for herself, because this woman knows how awful it is to be lonely all day and have men interested while one's youth is ebbing away. Nin tells this older friend she loves Guiler and knows he would never forgive. She then writes that she can use her imagination to avoid an affair because she is willing to "wait" for her husband.

Nin tries to find her value, whether it be through her writing or through her ability to interest men. Occasionally she comes down to earth and thinks about material matters. Thus, realizing that writing is her most tangible skill, Nin tries to find work to supplement her husband's income. She pursues a job writing articles for a newspaper but is turned away, and then an agent rejects her stories for magazines. Instead of feeling deflated, Nin comes to believe the world simply does not understand her writing. She admits to her diary she's blowing herself up with a bit of "egoism."

And then Nin sends a canary into what could be a deadly coalmine. About her American friend, Kay, she writes, "I am directly responsible for her having a lover." Kay tells Nin, "Thank you for [D. H.] Lawrence." Anaïs wonders if she herself will

have the courage, the beauty and power to live it all through, the adultery and the playacting and the emotional splitting. There must be no feeling of wrongdoing, or cobwebby remorse, or the slightest timorousness, or the untrue interpretation of lying – if you think you lie, you lie. If you know what you are doing, you know the real meaning of lie; a lie is not something you tell others, but yourself.

Some months after the stock market crash, Guiler, who has made desperate attempts to salvage his savings, now accepts that he is "ruined." Nin admits to herself that though she had been proud of her life, she now realizes it was money and her husband's work that made it possible. The couple moves out of the exotic apartment she had carefully designed and into a small country house far from the city she loves. It is a difficult move for Nin, but this is another secret. She writes, "I am ashamed of my unhappiness. Anyway, only my Journal knows it."

Away from the bustle of Paris, Nin creates another beautiful home, though a cozier and less glamorous one. But this turns out to be a gift in disguise, for Nin now has the quiet to really concentrate on her writing. She works hard, consciously forging her own style, but she has difficult time knowing when to listen to others' opinions about it. She's come to believe her diary is "a journal of consciousness" and admits the portraits she creates of people are much better than the reality. She then connects her writing to her longing, confessing, "My created image [is] something to reach out to ... capable of filling this unfillable craving in me."

Nin's relationship with her cousin Eduardo takes a turn when he tells her he's obsessed with her and they flirt with the idea of a romance. Nin writes, "human relationships are dangerous – because the mind has no power over them." Her view on lying also continues to evolve as she records in her diary, "I am beginning to lie to him to make things more interesting. We dramatize our lives – when it isn't naturally dramatic." Eduardo tells Nin she doesn't talk enough to "implicate" herself, but she believes when she does talk, others don't understand her; for this reason, she instead talks in her journal. She writes, "Love is an urge for what we do not possess." And then she tells her cousin an elaborate lie of a poor violinist who loves her: "Imaginary!" She goes on

What fun! ... And fundamentally, this satisfies me. These delusions and inventions do not weigh on me. Our relationship has been so enriched. What a woman [Eduardo] has known! (Nonexistent.) ... And the loveliest quality to my disguise is that I thus conceal again, as always, my true self.

By 1931, when Nin is 28 years old, she begins psychoanalyzing herself. To begin, she realizes she is making herself "strange" and people respond by leaving her out. She describes herself as excessively anxious, imagining negative things, feeling a sense of high drama, even fainting. She believes that if Sigmund Freud analyzed her, his diagnosis would be "sexual." Nin confesses to herself the "necessity I felt to be in love with Hugo and infatuated with someone else." Then she admits she believes it all stemmed from a desire for Erskine. She has "cleaned up [her] conscience," she writes, by admitting the obsession. She believes she has an inferiority complex because of being a girl, a sickly child, and badly dressed in school. Nin then thoroughly recounts her sexual "awakening," which seemed to come late but started with childhood romanticism. She claims her husband is the only one who's really stirred her, but she writes that Guiler has been restrained, frightened, and has idealized her too much, which has led to her frustration. She confesses she's asked her husband to treat her less delicately and his reaction was relief; she believes this new start "may save" their marriage. She believes having Erskine "repudiate" his attraction for her was damaging. And Nin then records in her diary that Guiler has admitted to painful secrets, too, specifically of suffering deep shame about being beaten as a child after displaying normal sexual curiosity.

Finally, Nin tip-toes close to revealing her "top secret" to her husband. Guiler tells her he knows she was attracted to Erskine, and she admits to the attraction – but no more. "I am strong enough to live with my secrets," she tells her diary. She then admits to her diary that her sex life with Guiler got off to an exceedingly slow start after they wed, due to his nervousness and fear. She states he was weak and she mothered him. Amazingly, Nin and Guiler discuss this and both believe the sexual reticence on his part led her to be attracted to Erskine. She finally discloses to her diary the desire to get away from her husband and his "unhealthiness." She writes she had once believed her diary had taken the place of Catholic confession, but has come to understand it was written from false premises. She now believes in the power of psychology, something that will stay with her for the rest of her life.

Indulging in self-analysis has opened the couple to a new honesty – and a new acceptance of Parisian "sensuality." Nin records in her diary that she and her husband have discussed having a "whim" outside of marriage. They also admit the belief that she leads him intellectually (which hurts her). Nin tells her diary she had been deeply disappointed because her husband had no originality in him. They joke about having affairs and keeping them secret so as to enjoy them without hurting each other. Nin imagines feeling attracted to a woman who is the opposite of herself. She believes she has suffered "intellectual and physical starvation" as a result of not having a father. At last, she connects that feeling of longing, hunger, and starvation to her obsession with Erskine.

In September 1931, Nin and Guiler travel to New York where she knows she will encounter John Erskine. On the boat she is terrified, even suicidal. Finally, after so much agony, a climactic moment: the couple arrives in New York and she sees Erskine, who again explains his belief that his "moment" with Nin was derailed by his thinking of Guiler. Nin realizes Erskine is not interested in her love for him, so her feelings start to dissipate. At this point, two of Nin's most important discoveries come to a head. For one, she entertains the belief that her journal may always be her best work. For another, she has come to believe in relationships outside of marriage, but for her husband, too.

At last, Nin reveals her "top secret" to her husband, telling him of the kiss with Erskine. Amazingly, she writes they both feel relieved of the burden of a falsely ideal marriage. Nin admits to her husband she had felt suicidal on the boat and Guiler makes her promise never to break up their marriage. Nin writes, "I am in my Journal, and in my Journal only, nowhere else. Nothing shows on the outside. Perhaps I do not exist except as a fantastic character in this story."

Nin needs resolution with the one who hurt her, the avatar for her father. She meets Erskine one last time and tells him she has a lover, which is a bold lie. She writes in her diary that since she and Guiler have discussed the possibility of taking lovers, it does not matter that it hasn't actually happened. Then, in a stunning reveal, Nin tells Erskine this extravagant untruth: that her new lover is Aldous Huxley, the renowned novelist. "Inside myself I was laughing," she writes. Upon hearing this "secret," Erskine encourages Nin to leave Guiler and live with Huxley. Nin replies that she loves her husband, wants to live with him, and is fine with "complexity" and "duality." Erskine then says he wishes it was him, puts his hand on her knee, holds her hand, compliments her, and speaks freely about his faults. Nin's lie has had the desired effect: "I could see that, from Aldous on, I would become infinitely more interesting. Inside myself I was laughing, laughing." Erskine puts his hand around her waist, displaying interest and no longer concerned with Guiler. But, signaling she is lost to him, Nin formally shakes his hand, ladling out the subtle rejection that puts her back in the power seat. (Interestingly, this is something she would later play out with her father: revenge for his having put her through hell.) She writes:

> And I, so pleased with my deviltry, realizing that most people love to be lied to, that imagination heightens life, that whenever there is a gap, or a little lukewarm condition I can start the play going again. That even an imaginary lover gave me a color which my idealism did not have, and gave John an interesting three hours. I left New York amused, elated, happy and blue, too, sorry to leave such a nice John. That to me was an artistic finish, a glossy one, you might say. It did me a lot of good to have something to flourish. Before that, things had been a bit flat. He never liked me better (next to our hour in Paris) than when I flourished Aldous.

Later, Guiler tells his wife he wishes she had had an experience with Erskine. Finally, Nin tells him the full story of Erskine's kiss, with his faltering because of thoughts of his friend, but of her willingness to go through with it. Incredibly, her husband says he pities and understands her. They make love, which for her is one of her best moments with Hugh Guiler. She writes of feeling greatly relieved. Her husband encourages her to write it all down because "this would make an extraordinary story." They both realize how much they had lionized the great novelist, John Erskine.

Nin and her husband have a new understanding. For one, they realize they had misunderstood each other because of their own wounds. "We did not know each other, and we were seeking each other for eight years," she writes. They feel their marriage is renewed and Nin feels "Bliss, bliss, bliss." It is a real high: "Everything is new. Our love is new; Hugh is new. Life is so rich. It is a high adventure."

*　*　*

Anaïs Nin's incredible relationship to secrets and lies was born during this passage of her mid-twenties. Though she did not yet know it, these secrets and lies would soon be part of her every day existence, becoming more and more labyrinthian. This is because, as *Volume Four* of Anaïs Nin's early diary ends, she is weeks away from meeting a man who would not only think highly of her writing, but also suffer no reservations about entering into an adulterous affair. He would be a nearly-starving but boldly talented novelist named Henry Miller.

BECOMING HERSELF

Childhood is believed by some to conclude at the end of one's twenties. Astrology makes much of Saturn's return when one is 28. Science reveals we are physically remade on a cellular level every seven years, meaning we're renewed as we approach our thirtieth year. And when Nin entered this moment of her journey, she began down an exciting and dangerous new path.

The diary Nin began writing in 1931 when she was 28 years old eventually awarded her worldwide fame, for this phase of her life was especially interesting. But while living this period, she felt forced to conceal the truth and kept her journals in a locked closet. Ironically, during these years, in many ways, Nin truly became herself.

Here are essays exploring Nin's life in the 1930s and '40s: an analysis of Nin's psychology in relation to Henry and June Miller; an examination of Nin's motivations in her relationship with her father; an argument about Nin as femme fatale; the introduction I wrote for Mirages *(the diary of Nin's self-described "nymphomaniac" phase); and an exploration of the psychologically stabilizing role of writing during this turbulent time in Nin's life.*

Shadow Selves

When she finally secured a deal to publish her diaries in the 1960s, Nin chose to begin in medias res with the early 1930s journal, the one in which she recorded her first impressions and ensuing relationship with Henry and June.

Meeting the glamorous Bohemian couple in December of 1931 was, for Nin, a dramatic moment. She was living in Louveciennes, a sleepy suburb on the outskirts of Paris, and this had given her the time and quiet to write. She was also eight years into her marriage to Hugh Guiler and hungry for new experience. Thus, when Henry and June appeared on her doorstep they acted as highly stimulating catalysts.

Nonconformist Henry and opaque, metamorphic June beautifully played the role of Nin's shadow, her dark self. They represented the part of herself she had repudiated – and yet she felt an irresistible attraction to them. They ignited Nin's desire to caretake and heal, as well as seduce, trick, create, and martyr herself. But Nin also sought to change them by making them respectable, generously giving the near-penniless couple her own typewriter, as well as money, clothes, understanding, and unfailing support. In this way she sought to nurture and champion forlorn aspects of herself through the Millers.

Henry Miller's gift to Nin was to help her relinquish her false, romanticized self by pulling her away from constant introspection and into "reality." This involved even the curbing of her diary writing, a habit that allowed her to live in a cocoon of dreams. The first volume of *The Diary of Anaïs Nin* reveals that she credited Miller with "saving" her from her addiction. She wrote triumphantly:

I accepted life as it is, the ugliness, the inadequacies, the ironies, for the sake of joy, for the sake of life. It is a comedy. It is slightly ridiculous and full of homeliness. ... Today I laughed. I let others care. I shift the burden. ... When a caring ceases, when one no longer struggles to build solidly, indestructibly, no longer erects cathedrals of faithfulness to the past, cathedrals of emotions, when one enters the realms of laxity, areas of ironic indifference and resignation, letting life flow with a certain emotional negligence, one may attain states of nirvana, dreaminess, beatitudes of another kind.

And while Nin did not entirely relinquish her old tendency to retreat into fantasy, she developed the ability to temper it with practicality and humor.

Meanwhile, June had a mysterious and yet earthy presence that Nin found herself attracted to in several ways. Nin was demure and virginal, while the conniving, overtly sexual June seemed her opposite. Nin quickly saw in June a suppressed part of her own nature she was jubilant to retrieve. She described June as "our fantasy let loose upon the world. She does what others do only in their dreams. ... There is a fantastic courage in this, to live without laws, without fetters, without thought of consequence."

As Nin began escaping from the tyranny of her purity, she found the key in June. She described June as her ideal: a woman who has "a dark, husky voice, a full strong body, who has the vigor and endurance, can stay up all night and drink all day." For several months, Nin was under the influence of June as one might be under the influence of a drug:

I want to live only for ecstasy. Small doses, moderate loves, all half-shades, leave me cold. I like extravagances. Letters which give the postman a stiff back to carry, books which overflow from their covers, sexuality which bursts the thermometer. I am aware also that I am becoming June.

Ultimately, June helped Nin shed her early incarnations as Catholic child and virgin saint, and she was able to integrate her darker traits into her image of herself. Several years later, after having been psychoanalyzed by Otto Rank, Nin wrote with discernment about her relationships with people such as the Millers. She achieved an insight that, because it prevented her from romanticizing, criticizing, or mythologizing them, enabled her simply to understand their purpose in her life. *The Diary of Anaïs Nin, Volume Two 1934–1939* includes this entry:

> The ones who have traveled too far from their primitive self must retrace their steps and find it again. ... I subjugated my own nature so much I had to live it through others. ... I wanted so much to be an ideal person, wise and evolved, and of course I wasn't. I would not allow myself the freedom to be capricious, jealous, angry, selfish or irresponsible. I was bound by my ideal self. ... To breathe freedom I had to live close to my shadows, my primitive shadows. They lived it all out for me. Deeply, I approved them. The first steps toward freedom are defiant and awkward.

Nin acknowledged that some facets of her personality had been born of fear and suppression, and the discovery of dormant identities led to more unity and fulfillment. Fittingly, Nin came to embrace the theories of the analytical psychiatrist Carl Jung who taught that a system of personality could "proceed to individuate" only by moving out of the subconscious and into consciousness.

Because as a young person Nin had wanted to defeat tragedy by creating an ideal self, she "prevented acts of destruction from arising from [her] consciousness."

She came to realize, though, that instead of accepting the darkness within herself, she had related to the "dark person who [represented] this" and sought to face the shadowy part of herself through that person. Once Nin was able to admit to the false idealism that had narrowed her world, she began to heal and her world began to widen.

Breaking the Ultimate Taboo

The incest taboo is so old and so ingrained it's almost unmentionable – and yet, incest happens.

When I came upon Anaïs Nin's descriptions of what she said was a consensual adult sexual liaison with her father, I was staggered. Who the hell sleeps with their father? It turned out that Anaïs Nin did – but why? To understand Nin's possible motivations, first consider another 20th century female icon.

It is well-known Marilyn Monroe was an "illegitimate" child who never knew her father, but he was most certainly a man named Charles Stanley Gifford. Monroe and Gifford were, as they say, "dead ringers." Marilyn, born Norma Jeane, was shown Gifford's photo when she was a young girl and her child's mind related him to the great masculine star of the day, Clark Gable. As her lonely and traumatic childhood progressed, Norma Jeane was said to have fantasized about the glamorous daddy who would rescue her. Instead, her first husband, Jim Dougherty, claimed she once tried to call Gifford and he quickly hung up on her.

Did rejection by her father ignite in Norma Jeane the tremendous drive for love and attention that propelled her quest for movie stardom? Possibly. According to her first acting coach, Natasha Lytess, Monroe made at least one more attempt to contact her father. Charles Casillo reports in *Marilyn Monroe: The Private Life of a Public Icon* that Lytess and the then-famous starlet drove to Gifford's home near Palm Springs, discussing Monroe's "father issues" during the drive, but that Monroe became anxious and decided to call first before showing up on his doorstep. Lytess waited in the car while Monroe nervously made the call at a payphone. A moment later she returned to the car and told Lytess that Gifford had responded, "Call my lawyer" – and hung up on her. Lytess said the episode broke Monroe's heart.

Somehow, the never-acknowledged "illegitimate" Norma Jeane became a font of acting genius and a wildly charming personality in the form of the world's preeminent sex symbol, one with a little girl's voice and supposed innocence – the kind of voice and innocence that might appeal to a daddy. She also left a trail of luscious images that still enthrall us long after she died. Did her father's rejection fuel the ambition it took for Norma Jeane to attain the attention of the world, attention she had not received from him? Did devastating heartbreak give birth to extreme drive and creativity?

One winter in the mid-1950s Nin met Monroe. The occasion of their meeting was the glamorous opening of an ice cream shop in New York City. *The Diary of Anaïs Nin, Volume Six 1955–1966* describes the scene:

> It was decorated in the old-fashioned way, all in ice-cream colors, very fresh and icy, and filled with celebrities. Some press agent thought it would be amusing to invite both Marilyn Monroe and Jayne Mansfield. It was to the detriment of Jayne Mansfield. Marilyn arrived without make-up, fresh and glowing, and instead of posing to be admired, she looked at everyone with genuine interest, and when I was introduced she turned her full warm attention on me.

Both Monroe and Nin, possibly because of their childhood deprivations, developed exceptional personalities. Both were masters at making meaningful connections, at touching people's hearts. But Casillo writes in *The Private Life of a Public Icon* that in the intervening years since her father's rejections, Monroe had still not overcome the hurt – and it seems it had turned into something else:

> As an adult, still wanting to be rescued by a father, she would attempt to re-create him in the men in her life. At a Manhattan party Marilyn confessed that she longed "to put on a black wig, pick up her father in a bar, and make love to him. Afterward she would ask, 'How do you feel now to have a daughter that you've made love to?'"

So there it is: sex (or the fantasy of such) as revenge. I believe Monroe's apparent desire for retaliation through sex is a powerful clue as to Nin's possible motivations. Sex is seen here, not only as coupling, but also as conquering.

Social anthropologists theorize that the incest taboo stems from a risk of inbreeding, but also from a need to create new alliances through marriage to non-relatives so as to strengthen the tribe. But what if the father and daughter never had an alliance? What if they were separated for 20 years and are strangers to one another? Would they then seek to make an alliance? Is it possible that girls who've been traumatically separated from their fathers have a compulsion to "co-join" with them as adults? Kathryn Harrison's memoir, *The Kiss*, tells her story of reuniting with her absent father at age 20 and having an affair. A pattern seems to be developing.

We must also consider what Sigmund Freud introduced as the Oedipus Complex (for boys) or the Electra Complex (for girls). Freud believed children pass through a stage of normal psychological development during which they feel a kind of desire for the opposite sex parent and competitive hostility for the same sex parent. The term was actually taken from a play written 2,400 years ago by Sophocles, the Greek tragedian. *Oedipus Rex* is a dramatization of the incest taboo: the story of a king, Oedipus, who unknowingly kills his father and marries his mother. When Oedipus discovers the truth, he blinds himself.

But Anaïs Nin didn't blind herself. Instead, she told the story in her diary and it is essentially this: She had been separated from her father for 20 years. They planned to meet in an effort to get to know each other. He was Joaquin Nin y Castellanos, a Cuban pianist, composer, and member of the French Legion of Honor who was enjoying a successful career in Europe. He joked that his daughter was his fiancée. (And when, fourteen years previously, sixteen-year-old Nin had sent him a portrait of herself, he jested charmingly that she was his "betrothed.")

Father and daughter met at a hotel in Chamonix, France during the summer of 1933 when Nin was 30 and her father was 53. Photographs prove they bore an incredible resemblance – the proverbial "dead ringers." They were both artists and shared a number of significant character traits. The meeting was intense, intimate, and Joaquin Nin took the opportunity to tell his daughter his side of the story regarding the break-up of his marriage to her mother. As is revealed in *Incest: The Unexpurgated Diary of Anaïs Nin 1932–1934*, father and daughter admitted to feeling upset and confused by their powerful feelings for one another. They were strangers who shared 50% of their DNA, after all. And then the father said, "Let me kiss your mouth." Daughter wrote that she was "tortured by a complexity of feelings," "tempted – terrified and desirous," and then a brief affair began. And then, daughter ended the affair.

Strangely, I believe the incest experience with Joaquin Nin "put to bed," so to speak, Anaïs Nin's unresolved issues with her father. He continued to pursue her, via letter, but he was eventually divorced by his wealthy wife and forced to return to Cuba where he spent the rest of his life in greatly reduced circumstances. When his daughter published a book titled *House of Incest* in 1936 he was alarmed, even terrified. (He needn't have been. The book is Nin's surrealistic exploration of the subconscious mind, a prose poem about a dream.) Joaquin Nin died alone in Cuba in 1949. Anaïs Nin wrote that after everything, after believing her feelings for the man were absolutely dead, she still cried when she learned he had passed away.

When Nin's secret diary revealing her incest experience was published in 1992, the reaction was swift and harsh. A review in the *New York Times* was titled "Nin's Diary Reveals Troubled Life, Mind: Writer Shown as Highly Self-Absorbed." Nin's friends didn't want to believe Nin had actually slept with her father and suggested the diary entries were fantasies. Nin's beloved younger brother, Joaquin Nin-Culmell, was extremely upset about the publication of the book and believed her reputation was irrevocably damaged. These reactions from friends and loved ones are understandable, but I found it surprising that one of Nin's biographers, Deirdre Bair, questioned the veracity of Nin's story and thought it necessary to go to "distinguished analysts and therapists" – something I find hilarious – to confirm that such a thing as "adult onset incest" is possible.

Anaïs Nin didn't lie to her diary. She romanticized. She dramatized. And – like all of us – she needed to see herself as the heroic protagonist of her own story. But she did not lie to her diary. When I read her account of incest with her father, I knew it was true.

Joaquin Nin y Castellanos was Anaïs Nin's ultimate shadow self. For 30 long years, between his discarding of her as a child and her reuniting with him as a 30-year-old woman, she saw the shadow of his face every time she looked in a mirror, this man who she once said had "crippled" her family.

Anaïs Nin's incest with her father? I believe it was the ultimate revenge. She entranced him and then abandoned him. She left him longing for her, begging to see her just as she as child had longed for him. She also eventually became the vastly more successful of the two. And then, though the account of their liaison was published long after they were both dead, she posthumously ruined his reputation. Let me put it this way: many decades after your death, how would you like it if people remembered you, not for your life's work, but as the father of much more famous artist with whom you'd had an incestuous relationship?

Anaïs Nin as Femme Fatale

"Femme fatale" is a French term meaning, literally, "deadly woman." In my view, a femme fatale is a woman who has gone through hell. Perhaps she harbors a secret pain or experienced a traumatic childhood loss. As a result, she has become cynical and dangerous or has, at the very least, garnered a reputation for danger. Here I take an ironic and whimsical approach to the subject, but Nin seems to have, in many ways, truly filled the bill.

A sensitive Spanish girl, Anaïs Nin was abused and abandoned by her philandering father who ran off with one of his rich music students. Nin's devastated mother responded by bringing little Anaïs and her two brothers to America, though while on the boat Anaïs started composing a letter to lure her father back to his family. This letter was the first entry in what became her diary – an idealized picture of her life over which she labored for 63 years, a series of books that eventually made her famous.

Little Anaïs grew up and tried, really tried to be a good wife to her doting banker husband, Hugh, but an existential depression had already set in. The abandonment by her father was something from which she could never quite recover and her one respite was her diary. It was the vehicle through which she kept her fantasies alive, for it encapsulated her dreams of beauty and happiness and of being loved and adored. The truth, though, was that she was doomed to a life of longing for ideal love.

When as an adult Nin finally met her father again, she was shocked to discover that he hadn't a clue as to how he had devastated his children (ain't that the way?) and seemed incapable of even a shred of remorse. Anaïs realized beyond a shadow of a doubt that her father was a horrible and selfish man, hardly the idealized god she'd described in her diary. And so she did what any self-respecting femme fatale would do: she stomped his heart and abandoned him.

Then, in a fascinating twist, Anaïs Nin, the once hurt child, took on her father's persona as duplicitous seducer and creative dynamo. She had scores of lovers and finally became a bigamist, all the while chronicling her glamorous adventures in her journal. She also produced dozens of delicately beautiful prose pieces, even writing what are known as some of the most important works of modern female erotica, including *Delta of Venus* and *Little Birds*. Nin's diaries were eventually published to tremendous acclaim and she became the pied piper of a throng of followers all determined to imitate her example of "proceeding from the dream."

In recent years, as Nin's unexpurgated diaries describing her numerous affairs and erotic adventures have been published (per her instructions), she has been condemned by scandalized critics – a sure sign that she's entered the pantheon of legendary femme fatales.

A Phase of Many Lovers

This piece was originally published as the introduction for Mirages: The Unexpurgated Diary of Anaïs Nin 1939–1947.

Anaïs Nin's diary is a remarkable work of art. Because she believed "the topsoil of our personalities is nothing," her diary chronicles her interior life, the "uncensored dream, the free unconscious," and it unspools like a tickertape. It is a deeply personal document, one that not only reveals the psychological topography of one woman, but one that unveils something of the interior life of all women, all people.

This uncensored diary is particularly explosive. It will no doubt enflame the usual brigade of outraged moralists who have heaped scorn upon Nin for daring to live by her own moral code, write about her adventures, and then allow that writing to be published for all to read. The vitriol with which she has been attacked proves her diary hits a nerve, but as H. G. Wells said, "Moral indignation is jealousy with a halo."

We know that in the great experiment that was her life, Anaïs Nin did things few of us would admit – or even consider. Most of her secrets involved her sex life, an area women have fought to control on their own terms. Nin had what appears to have been an incredibly full and exciting life, but she believed she suffered from "neurosis" or "sickness" and she fought to understand its cause. In the meantime, and without even a high school education, Nin forged a modern art form that will finally find its place in this century of Internet communication, full as it is of personal confession. But Nin was decades and lightyears ahead, trailblazing the exploration of an area of human life so mysterious, so elemental, so beyond politics and social mores, so personal, and yet so universal. To Nin's detractors one must ask, "If one's lens is too small to fit the mysteries of one complex life, if that life must be condemned, what in the critic's own complex psyche do they condemn and attempt to destroy?"

Nin's story must begin with her father, Joaquin Nin, a respected Spanish composer who abused his children and then abandoned his family, leaving them nearly destitute while he married a wealthy young music student and toured in luxury throughout Europe. Nin, her mother, and two brothers were forced to sail for America in 1914 and, while on board the ship, eleven-year-old Anaïs began writing a letter to lure her father back to the family. This letter was never sent, but was the beginning of her diary – a letter to the world, a 63-year-long cry from the heart.

Mirages opens at the dawn of World War II when Nin fled Paris, where she lived for fifteen years with her husband, banker Hugh Guiler. She had married "Hugo" in 1923 and, though he loved her and she trusted him, she found the union deeply unsatisfying. In spite of this, the 1930s had been an idyllic period for her and she continued her diary. At a time when it was considered shocking for her to have done so, Nin wrote a book-length analysis of D. H. Lawrence's fiction, including the infamous *Lady Chatterly's Lover*, and it had been published. She also wrote a long, surrealistic prose piece entitled *House of Incest*.

In what proved to be a dramatic turning point in her life, Nin met writer Henry Miller and his wife June in 1931. As is detailed in Nin's first unexpurgated diary, *Henry and June*, Nin and Miller championed one another as writers and began an affair. Nin and Guiler also supported Miller financially and paid for the printing of his ground-breaking novel, *Tropic of Cancer*. Then in 1933, after a 20-year separation, Nin met her father again. Daughter and father were strangers, he a notorious Don Juan and she a 30-year-old woman. They fell into a brief, incestuous affair, which Nin unflinchingly described in her second unexpurgated diary, *Incest*. Shortly thereafter, Nin sought psychoanalysis from Otto Rank, a close colleague of Sigmund Freud, but he too fell in love with her and this story was revealed in the following unexpurgated diary, *Fire*. And in *Nearer the Moon*, Nin told the story of her intense relationship with Left Bank Marxist Gonzalo Moré, with whom she is still deeply involved at the outset of *Mirages*.

Mirages begins in 1939 with Nin's arrival in America and ends in 1947 when she meets the man who would be "the One," the lover who would satisfy her insatiable hunger for connection. In the middle looms a period Nin describes as "hell," during which she experiences a kind of erotic madness, a delirium that fuels her search for love. As a child suffering the loss of her father, little Anaïs wrote, "Close your eyes to the ugly things," and against a horrifying backdrop of war and death, Nin combats the world's darkness with her own search for light.

Mirages is just that: a series of mirages that dance tantalizingly on the road, one after another, promising refuge and water, but then cruelly evaporate like so many hopes and dreams. As with all artists, Nin's fodder was her feelings and she created from the vantage of shattering pain originating with her father's rejection. In this volume, Nin writes movingly of her "sickness," puts herself through repeated self- and professional analyses, and comes what seems perilously close to annihilation. In the end, this book serves as a 20th-century Persephone's journey through the underworld.

The reader who wishes to cross this particular desert with Nin must be willing to trust that an oasis will be found at the end. Finally, after meeting Rupert Pole in early 1947, Nin will enjoy a fulfilling relationship at last, one that will end her frantic search for love, though it will not conclude her story. Instead, she will then embark on a "trapeze" life in which she swings between Rupert Pole and Hugo Guiler for years – a nearly impossible feat and one of the most gripping periods in her story.

Out of abandonment, tremendous pain, and "great hunger," Anaïs Nin created a life-long work of art that is unparalleled, one that breaks the false barriers between fiction and non-fiction, diary and novel, conscious and unconscious, societally-sanctioned and the unsanctioned, public and private. It took courage for Nin to write about that which exists beyond words in an period of such censorship society demanded that fictional characters be seen paying for their "sins." She seemed to foresee what we today take for granted in the 21st century: that consciousness is a streaming tickertape of words and images spooling from us as long as we live, and something to be shared.

For those who dare to ride along the precipitous twists and turns of Anaïs Nin's fantastic story: proceed.

Writing Makes One Whole

For Nin, beginning a diary required the construction of a heroic protagonist, an idealized version of herself. But writing in her diary also led to the discovery of genuine aspects of her character that integrated to form a more authentic personality. She believed writing was the "strongest element in [her] divided and chaotic self," and said, "No matter what disintegrating influence I was experiencing, the writing was an act of wholeness."* Thus, Nin's diary serves as a unique document that chronicles the evolution, even revolution, of a personality. It reveals many of the dynamics of the process of retreating into constructed selves and the rediscovery of the true self.

Nin was not alarmed that she had lived out multiple personae, because she believed "you cannot reach unity and integration without patiently experiencing first all of the turns of the labyrinth of falsities and delusions in which man has lost himself."† She knew the individual is always in a process of becoming and the order humans seek is within them. She believed there is a unity and oneness that contains the constant transformations and aspects of the self. And this unity is echoed in the largest and smallest facets of life.

Ultimately, Nin revealed a sense of wonder regarding her exhaustive search for her true character, as well as a profound respect for the miraculous workings of the psyche. In finally eschewing aesthetics, order, and the ideal, she was awakened. Ironically, it was in this supposed chaos

---

* Nin, Anaïs. *In Favor of the Sensitive Man.* New York: Harcourt, Brace and Jovanovich, 1976.

† Nin, Anaïs. "The Writer and the Symbols." *Two Cities: The Revue Bilinque de Paris* 5, 1969.

that she found a mysterious order and wisdom. An entry in the second published volume of her diary states:

> Fulfillment is the completion of a circle. All aspects of the self have to be lived out, like the twelve houses of the zodiac. A personality is one who has unrolled the ribbon, unfolded the petals, exposed all the layers. It does not matter where one begins: with instinct or wisdom, with nature or spirit. The fulfillment means the experience of all parts of the self, all the elements, all the planes. It means each cell of the body comes alive, awakened. It is a process of nature, and not of the ideal. One dies when the cells are exhausted, one reaches plentitude when they all function, the dream, desire, instinct, appetite. One awakens the other. It is like contagion. The order does not matter. All the errors are necessary, the stutterings, the blunders, the blindesses. The end is to cover all the terrain, all the routes. ... To live only one aspect or one side of the personality is like using only one sense, and the others become atrophied. There is greatness only in fulfillment, in the fullness of awaking. Completion means the symphony. Sublimation means to condemn to immobility certain members of the body for the sake of the monstrous development of others. ... Psychologically, a great personality is a circle touching something at every point. A circle with a core. A process of nature, growth, not the ideal. The ideal is an error. Life is a full circle, widening until it joins the circle motions of the infinite.

While diary writing made evident Nin's construction of a self, it also revealed why its creation was necessary and helped to expose various facets of that self. Perhaps most importantly, diary writing helped Nin realize that she need not "remain in bondage" to her first experience, first relationship, and first vision of herself. She was able to smash the "deforming mirror" and experience wholeness and joy.

MID-LIFE COMPLICATIONS

Researching the middle period of Nin's life, the time during which she somehow managed multiple secret relationships, necessitated diving into the Nin papers held at UCLA, as well as private documents stored in her home. I pored through hundreds of unpublished diary pages, letters, and notes, finding incendiary material that had been hidden for decades.

The first chapter of this section, "When Her Husband Took a Stand," is based on unpublished letters I discovered in Nin's files. This is the first time Nin's husband, Hugh Guiler, has been given a voice – and it finally solves a mystery.

The author and wit Gore Vidal famously hated Nin and I wanted to know why. The second chapter of this section, "Gore Vidal's Secret Proposal," exposes the truth of their relationship, revealing the real reason Vidal smeared Nin and perpetrated a cover-up of his feelings for her.

This section also reveals, through my discovery of raw diary pages, the truth about Nin's bi-coastal marriages. I wanted to know how she managed two husbands and how she kept them secret from one another. I found the answer hidden in the files.

This section concludes with my previously unpublished introduction to Trapeze: The Unexpurgated Diary of Anaïs Nin 1947–1955. *Having helped prepare the manuscript for publication, I was asked to contribute the book's introduction so as to give my insights on this period of*

Nin's life. I received a note from the editor disputing my statement that society has derided openly sexual women. I did not care to dilute my assertion, so my introduction was left unpublished. A short time later, a movement of female outrage against such blindness exploded on social media. And so, "Step Right Up: The True-Life Story of Anaïs Nin's Amazing Life on the Trapeze" is published here for the first time.

When Her Husband Took a Stand

He wrote the letter in the late 1940s, his handwriting tight and masculine, his words clear and direct. He begins:

> There is no use you coming back to New York until I work this thing out further with myself. I believe now the truth is, and there is no use concealing it from each other under a lot of words, that I have been angry at a whole accumulation of things in our relationship, and you have been too.

For me, these words come as a lightning bolt, a sighting as electrifying as Captain Ahab's of *Moby Dick*. Hugh Guiler was the seemingly long-suffering husband who existed as an almost spectral presence in Anaïs Nin's unexpurgated diaries and was nonexistent in her expurgated diaries, appearing only briefly as the artist "Ian Hugo." Yet, Guiler was the one to whom Nin remained attached for nearly 54 years, despite her relationships with other men. Could it be this most mysterious of husbands had left his own written record of feelings about his complicated marriage? Could it be that Guiler, the famously cuckolded mate, the comically portrayed and much-pitied character, was not the spectacular dupe he seemed?

To read the diaries of Anaïs Nin was for me – as it is for many others – to feel that I had entered an intense and personal relationship with a woman who had been dead for years. It was also to feel I had entered into relationships with the many "characters" that populate her diary – especially the enigmatic Guiler (or "Hugo," as she calls him). I came across Nin's first journal, her "childhood" diary, when I was an undergrad studying literature and found it beautiful, educational, and inspirational. I went on to read all of her diaries sequentially. The story of her life unfolded before me, a winding scavenger hunt for clues packed with hair-pin turns and dramatic leaps.

Nin had married Hugh Guiler in 1923 when she was 20 and he was 25. She wrote of their relationship so beautifully it was hard not to fall in love with her sensitive, gentlemanly mate, but six years into her marriage it became clear Nin was dissatisfied and desperate. One of my first shocks occurred when, while reading *The Early Diary of Anaïs Nin, Volume Four*, I came upon the entry in which Nin described her first dalliance with a man other than her husband. She then began a long search for her "real love." In 1947 Nin met Rupert Pole and they entered a relationship that lasted until her death in 1977. In the meantime, though, Nin remained married to Guiler and lived what she described as life on a "trapeze," swinging precariously between Guiler (who lived on the east coast) and Pole (who lived on the west coast).

As I read Nin's diaries I became adept at "forgiving" Anaïs, for sometimes her descriptions of her life taxed my admittedly tolerant world-view. I accepted and accept her in totality, just as I accept John Lennon (a god-awful father to Julian), or Picasso (a dreadful womanizer), or Hemingway (a cruel "friend" to a vulnerable F. Scott Fitzgerald). I accept Anaïs Nin's betrayals of her husband because, as D. H. Lawrence said, a soul is "a dark forest." And if a soul is a dark forest, a marriage must be an ocean, a mystery, a landscape full of creatures in its shadows.

Still, one of my continual, nagging questions was "What about Hugh?" It's a conundrum, for in spite of my admiration of Nin's writing and acceptance of her as a complex human being, I came to feel protective toward her husband. I liked him. I wanted him to be happy. I wanted him to stand up, to fight for his dignity. And perhaps this is also what Anaïs Nin wanted. Guiler's seeming non-response to Nin's relationship with Rupert Pole (I hesitate to use the word "bigamy," though that's what it eventually became) was hard to take. When I spent time with Pole many years later, the subject of Hugh Guiler arose. Over a Mexican dinner, Pole, an exceedingly genteel man, dismissed his rival with prickly finality, a simple guillotine swipe. For Pole, Guiler was "just a banker" – as if that door was firmly closed.

But it wasn't closed for me. Guiler had once written that, in response to having been planted in Anaïs Nin's "garden," he had produced his own "green leaves." In fact, Guiler made at least fifteen experimental films, as well as etchings and engravings. He also traveled the world and was relocated by his employer from New York to Paris in the mid-1920s and then back to New York at the beginning of World War II. Surely this intelligent, worldly man had a voice. So when his marriage to Nin started to crack, did Guiler know? Did he suffer? Wasn't he angry – angry enough to do something? Or did Guiler have secrets all his own?

I sought information from the period of 1949, for my intuition told me this was possibly a momentous year – one in which Nin's relationship with Pole had most definitely taken root. Within a folder of Nin's papers for that year I found a long diary entry by Nin written in April and a long letter written by Guiler in December. These documents provide powerful clues as to the dynamics of the Nin/Guiler marriage, their individual positions, and – for perhaps the first time – Hugh Guiler's stand.

"A Night of Fog"

Nin's diary entry from this period, written in large, looping blue ink on loose pages and dated "April 15 – 1949," describes her "real life" with Rupert in San Francisco. She writes that she lives "like a typical American wife," getting up at 6:30 in the morning, pulling on her "slacks and sweater," and sending Rupert off to work. Several hours later the mailman arrives, bringing a long letter from Guiler, Nin's legal husband. Nin then describes her dilemma:

> Our relationship [with Hugh] is for me a playing for time, an edifice of lies, a postponement – I won the last game – He returned to NY April 1 and I expected to have to go to see him but managed by infinite intricacies to postpone home coming until June because he is going to France in May – In June Rupert will have a summer job where I can't be with him. I can't desert him [Hugh] altogether, and I can't leave Rupert.

Nin describes what is for her the difference between the two relationships. About Rupert she writes, "The love I feel is deep," while she bemoans an obligatory visit to Hugh: "I owe Hugh that." With Rupert she has become "peacefully domestic – because the peace, the monotony of house work is broken by our wild love making, our lyrical, stormy, lightning caresses," but her husband and the failure of their relationship weigh heavily on her mind:

> Every day I question the mystery of my physical life with Hugo – What happened? What destroyed it? Was it [his] inexperience and mine? Was it inadequacy on his part? Was it dissatisfaction [and] sensual unfulfillment which

estranged me from him? Now that I have this fulfillment with Rupert, I have become faithful, domestic. I can sew, mend, repair, repeat, clean, wash – because there will be a climax, a lyrical moment, a sensation, a certitude of high living. The high living moment must have been absent from my marriage, because I had always the feeling I was trapped away from such experience, waiting, en marge, with Hugo ... [Nin's ellipses] that this high moment lay outside, in the night, in the absent lover ... [Nin's ellipses] Poor Hugo – What could he do? Sometimes I tried, delicately, to impart what I had learned, but his manhood rebelled there – Our love making was tragic – ineffectual –

A night of fog – Music on the radio – Leave the past alone.

Nin goes on to describe her intense unhappiness at having to entertain Guiler's bank clients in his and Nin's luxurious apartment. Guiler had given Nin "brilliant multicolored Chinese dolls" that delighted her; she places one of these dolls in full view of their guests in a symbolic effort to make the occasion bearable, but she finds the guests "cold, arrogant." She later writes, "Hugo thought he had married a woman. I can be chic. I can look aristocratic. I have beautiful manners – But I am unhappy and strained." She longs to be with Rupert, for "Rupert and I seek our pleasure, more humble ones, we avoid ordeals, we live by our wishes, we go alone to skii [sic], we go to the movies, we seek those we like," but then she adds, plaintively,

But it is Hugo who bought me the dolls –
Around, around, around, a circle of madness. Dependence. Rebellion – Refaction [sic] – Guilt – A child like dependency – I cannot grow in that direction –
I cannot grow in arrogance, in a hard finish, in a gold plated irony, impertinence, cynicism of the wealthy[.]

Nin writes that in examining the situation with her therapist, she "obessionally fought to be just to Hugo, to eliminate the neurotic obstacles of our marriage, to save Rupert from the tragedy of an impossible marriage." Still, she cannot escape the difference between Guiler and Pole and she describes why she believes she is happier with Pole:

> Hugo could endure monotony, discipline, daily repetitions, meals at the same hour – Every unpredictable change, every variation disturbed him. After I cook and wash dishes with regularity for a week, if I hint lightly to Rupert: I'm tired of dishes, let's go out to dinner, he is not only eager for a change, but more often it is he who will suddenly drop his work, and say to me: we're off – I have barely time to don my coat, the car is already pulsating, there is a mood of freedom, a breaking of bonds, of halters, harnesses, a sudden influx of speed and lightness – Poor Hugo –
>
> I am hoping he is now learning to live more happily without me.

It seems Nin's choice is clear: her desire – or so it appears – is to live full-time with Rupert Pole. She admits to feeling "lonely in the world" unless she is with him, because then she is "at ease. Satisfied. The world is complete – Where ever my lover is, the world is complete." She describes their spiritual and symbolic "marriage" as having taken place "long ago in Denver, on the sand dunes." She describes it as "love-making [that] contained all we were, are, would be" and wrote, with finality, that with this "marriage," finally, "gravity is achieved." Meanwhile, though, Guiler's letters express an adoration for Nin so intense that, as she explains to her diary, she simply can't bear to leave him altogether.

"A Soul of My Own"

Hugh Guiler lived what must have been a puzzled, puzzling existence in New York City, separated for long periods from the wife he appeared to love deeply. Surely he must have known – or at least suspected – she had another lover or lovers. But how can we know, hearing as we do only the voice of Nin?

I found an answer to this mystery in a 23-page letter written by Guiler on "Sunday 12/4/49," one that clearly, for once, reveals his state of mind. It seems to be one of the few missives Guiler wrote to his wife that does not begin with an affectionate salutation, such as "Darling." Instead he begins this communication abruptly, soon going on to state:

> There is no use [illegible] coming back to New York until I work this thing out further with myself. I believe now the truth is, and there is no use concealing it from each other under a lot of words, that I have been angry at a whole accumulation of things in our relationship, and you have been too. We admire each other, we have pity for each other but in our actual actions & attitude towards each other we have both shone [sic] that for the time being at least anger is stronger than the other emotions. As long as that lasts we are going to make each other unhappy when we are together and I for my part do not want to inflict this on you any more until my anger disappears.

And thus begins what is a long cry from the heart, one that appears to lay Guiler's cards on the table in a way he was unable previously, one in which much of the dynamic between himself and his famous wife seems to be, finally, made plain.

The question as to whether Nin and Guiler had entered into an "open marriage" is dispelled when Guiler makes a brief reference to it, reminding his wife of her reaction to his "taking another woman." This creates a new understanding, for if Nin and Guiler had agreed on a non-monogamous relationship then many of Nin's affairs could not be considered betrayals of her husband. Interestingly, though, Guiler writes that because of her angry response to his brief affair, he doubts Nin's love altogether. Could it be Guiler knowingly tolerated Nin's affairs, but then was surprised to discover that the same tolerance was not extended to him?

Over and over in this long letter Guiler states he is angry, as if for the first time coming to grips with this most common of emotions. "That is the fact," he writes, "and I think it is all wrong for me to cover up under a lot of fine literature & protestations the central fact that I am angry." But then he reveals an impediment to his being able to express his anger: "[Y]ou cannot stand anger in me. Well, I am angry and you will feel my anger, as well as my other tender feelings, if you come to New York now, as I believe I have felt yours."

With great insight, Guiler perceives one of Nin's central struggles: the "splitting conflict," as he calls it.

> I appreciate the great effort you have made to solve the problem by capitulating (as you think it is) [illegible] the life you want & coming to New York. But every sign indicates that you cannot do this without a splitting conflict, even to wait until my analysis is finished, and will on your part, in spite of every effort to the contrary, result in unconscious acts that show your own real angers.

Again describing their mutual anger and also providing vivid clues to the methods with which they've attempted to explain away their problems, Guiler writes,

And there is no need to fool ourselves that these angers on both sides are all out of the past. ... You began to deal with this honestly when you said there are certain sides of me you just don't like & have no feeling for at all. That is today & not the past.

Finally, Guiler gets down to brass tacks, the practical but puzzling truths of their marriage, the elephants in their well-decorated room. How did Nin and Guiler explain to themselves the fact that they did not live together for much of the time? These long separations are what gave Nin the means to pursue intensive extra-marital relationships, but how had they negotiated this arrangement? Guiler begins by reminding Nin, "You have needed to absent yourself for periods in order to find yourself," and then goes on to detail the situation:

... I now realize we have always been under cover of one excuse or another, arranging to be apart a good deal of the time, except during the war years when we could not do otherwise .... The truth is we were not together more than momentarily & spasmodically for the years between 1928 (when I took over the trust work in Paris & started traveling, with your approval & encouragement "to preserve the marriage" you used to say) while I had the Trust Debt in Paris I traveled I suppose about 6 months out of each year. Then I went to London Jan. of 1938 and you took the decision not to accompany me so I paid for only weekend visits about once or twice a month over the next year & a half. We did not do this to "preserve the marriage" but because we were too unhappy living with each other all the time. I probably fooled myself about this more than you did, as I am sure your diary shows. The periods of being together were therefore also charged with exaggerated feelings in an effort to make up for what each of us thought we had been depriving the other of in the intervening period, or what we thought we had the right to receive because we had been deprived of something.

Having examined these facts and realizing many of their separations have occurred under of the guise of Nin's stated desire to "find" herself, Guiler states unequivocally, "Now I need to find myself."

Guiler then squarely faces what he has come to understand as his predominant weakness, one Nin laments in her unexpurgated diaries and one any astute reader of Nin will sense:

> The greatest problem I have & one which has created a big problem for you also, (accentuated by your need to have someone dependent on you spiritually, you in turn being dependent in other ways) – is my over-dependence on you. In this respect I have been like a child & now after 51 years of childhood, or reversion to childhood, I must have some time & learn how to go out myself, make friends myself without you, and to acquire a whole new attitude that is not at every turn simply another road around you.

And here Guiler shows a deep empathy for his wife's plight:

> You have asked me a hundred times. "Why are you so dependent on me? Why do you have no world of your own? Why don't you know what you want? – colors in this apartment or anything else concerning our personal life? Why don't you express yourself directly instead of always through me? Why do I always have to be your soul? (You were really saying, while saying in words that you were my soul) Have you no soul of your own?" (you really were asking)
>
> All that was in part true and I have at last awakened to it & all it implies. It has been a terrible burden for you

to carry even when [illegible] you said you liked carrying it and so often said that you were my soul. In the last year or two you have been trying to tell me that you could no longer carry that burden & now I understand I agreed with you really when I took up the analysis, which represented my effort to carry my own responsibilities.

But then when, as a result of analysis, a soul of my own did start to appear and you began to see the shape of it, you were taken aback. It was not what you had imagined, not what you had wished for – or at least only in part, and it was then that a more serious withdrawal took place on your part.

Having faced and come to grips with his failings, Guiler then describes his discovery of his real self. He writes that he is a businessman who creates art avocationally, one who does not share his wife's all-consuming interest in the arts and artists. He explains how he came to this understanding:

Bogner [Guiler's and Nin's analyst] has only last week broken the news to me that I have been deceiving myself as to thinking that I am an artist. She says I am obviously primarily a business man and only secondarily, and on the side, an artist. It came as a great shock to me but I believe she is right. Much of my artistic endeavor was due to my despising myself as a business man & feeling that I had to prove in some other way that I had a soul. But the business world represented reality for me and, to the extent that my artistic activities were done in the spirit of a flight from reality the forms they took could not be otherwise than exaggeratedly remote, introspective and inhuman. Then on the business side there were corresponding tensions & exaggerations because such activities were under constant attack from within (myself) and from without (by you).

Guiler explains that he in fact enjoys business, finds it "inspirational & imaginative," and would also like to pursue his interest in "the movies." With great enthusiasm, he also describes his enjoyment of making money and then says, with finality,

> And I will probably continue to keep up this combination of unenslaved, flexible business activities & movies, as well as my general interest in art, for the rest of my days because that is me.

Having admitted to his own faults and having defined a self, Guiler then focuses on Nin and what he believes are her failings. He begins by explaining that he enjoys knowing some artists because he likes "many of them as human beings, and I want them as well as others to like my movies." But in a statement that strikes at the heart of his wife's chief vice, Guiler writes:

> I am not going to take their opinion as final because I have found from experience that so called artistic judgments often conceal neurotic liars.

He goes on to conduct an astute analysis of his wife that also seems a refutation of her claims against him:

> The artist ... sometimes [has] something valuable to contribute & at other times simply [sits] behind his own kind of defensive barriers, except that he has the nerve to claim that they have something sacred & privileged about them that must be given special consideration. Everyone, I believe, is out for power and achievement in different ways and you today, for example, are just as ambitious to [illegible] your books as I am to [illegible] through my business. What is unfair, I think, is that you have tended to act as if your ambitions were in some way exercised for more noble & lofty aims than mine in business. That I now reject completely and I believe you

are honest enough, when you really think about it, to do the same. ... Childhood neuroses often compel you to act differently from what you really believe.

But you are what you are and certainly I am not the one to criticize your ambition to have a successful career of power & achievement, for I have nothing against that. I realize this furthermore is a structure which has been built up from your earliest days and that is something very real to you, and assumes an importance in your life so great that you feel you have to defend it at all costs.

Then, in a somewhat convoluted fashion, Guiler makes his most pointed claim against his wife. He describes her behavior as arising from:

dissociation in yourself from one kind of business in order to carry on another kind, that the kind of business you chose did not feed you & that you therefore had to take from the one you dissociated yourself from to support the other.

In short, while disparaging Guiler's work as a banker and while also lauding the supposedly superior life of the artist, Nin utilized Guiler's earnings to pursue the arts. She also used Guiler's money to support her artist friends and lovers. And though he may soften this stunning accusation with vague words, it is clear Guiler was not and had not been in the dark about the seemingly subterranean activities of his wife.

And so, after many years of marriage and many blows to his dignity, Hugh Guiler asserted himself at last. It is clear he was aware of what I and so many readers discovered while reading Anaïs Nin's diaries: she and Guiler were two people at rather tragic odds. Guiler faces this fact without self-pity and gives Nin the ultimate out, one without strings:

The question you must ask yourself is whether you want to continue to be married to the person I have presented to you as my real self – whether you can continue in such a marriage without the unhappiness that has resulted from each of us keeping before us a false & unreal picture of the other.

He describes his new attitude as one that has occurred upon "waking up," seemingly from a somnambulistic state, from a "series of shocks":

But you see, darling, I have had a great shock, really from waking up suddenly & realize that during my sleep I have been subjected to a long series of shocks and I must have some time to gather myself together & gain new strength in myself, so that I will no longer be angry, as I will be as long as confidence has not returned, which will take time after such a violent upheaval. ... You still write in the sense of being compelled to pay up for something and I do not feel that you will be alright with yourself or with me until this has changed into something more positive; until you really feel that the two businesses (whether the two between us, or the two in yourself) are ready to go hand in hand towards a common goal, rather than one hand must pay for having taken bank notes out of the other.

For I am now completely disposed to accept the facts as we have discovered in each other ... [and] any forcing at this time will only make it impossible for us ever to work out a relationship on a new and realistic basis.

Finally, in an electrifying passage, one that dissolves the long-held myth perpetuated by Nin that she was forced to live her life on the "trapeze" because her husband couldn't let her go, Guiler then signals to his beloved wife that she may gently cut the ties between them:

I think it may be best for you to consider San Francisco as your headquarters and your stays in New York as visits only. As I get back into the foreign field I will be spending

more & more time in Brazil & Mexico on business ....
We can then see how much time the demands of our
respective careers permit us to be together.

And there it was: the open door through which Nin could
walk. It must've taken tremendous courage for Guiler to
turn that knob and open the way to true separation and
divorce. Then, in a kind of post mortem, he locates a core
of insecurity between them:

> We never had the peace that comes from being sure that
> each of us was accepted for himself & herself. Always a
> state in which that self was threatened.
>
> So now Anaïs I know you for what you are and you
> know me for what I am. There is no need for either of
> us to make the slightest demands on the other. When I
> get a little more on my feet I will not feel threatened any
> more and I have no desire to take away from you your
> individuality as an artist or a woman, or do anything but
> give the fullest reins to your career. Let us expect little of
> each other & perhaps we will get something. And I assure
> you there will be no more ultimatums on my part if there
> are none on yours.

Here the letter ends abruptly as it appears the final page
has been lost, but what remains dramatically contradicts
the picture Anaïs Nin painted of being tragically caught
between two men: one she loves and the other who
exists as an obligation. This letter of December 1949
proves Guiler gave Nin an opportunity to live full-time
with Rupert Pole. How did Nin respond? Guiler's next
correspondence tells the tale:

> I felt after hearing the lift in your voice yesterday over
> the telephone that we have definitely passed the crisis
> and I am so glad we can take the vacation in Mexico as
> a beginning of a new life. ...

And this is signed:

> Love, new love
> The new, new love H.

The next communication? A postcard from the Grand Canyon addressed from Nin to Guiler:

> Dear Monkey
> A wonderful trip spent on looking back as our wonderful three weeks of real joyous expansion together – the fruit of our joint efforts. Feel happy and light.
>
> Your woman
> A.

And so it stands. Hugh Guiler gave Anaïs Nin the opportunity to leave him, to divorce, to step off the "trapeze." He did not hold her; instead, he clearly stated he had a life, goals, and "a soul of his own." But for reasons of her own, Nin would not, could not, did not let him go. She chose to continue her dual relationships with Guiler and Rupert Pole until the end of her days.

For me, Hugh Guiler's letter creates a new understanding. I now believe that Anaïs Nin was not so much caught between two adoring men, but was a woman caught within her own need to create and maintain opposing forces that would nearly tear her in two. In the end, Nin's diaries are a letter to the world, a confession, an on-going cry for understanding and, perhaps, forgiveness. They have secured her place in literary history and have made famous many of the "characters" they describe. But let it be known that for at least one powerful moment, Hugh Guiler took a stand.

Gore Vidal's Secret Proposal

"You are quite necessary to me as you know."

— Gore Vidal

For years I'd wondered about the relationship between Gore Vidal and Anaïs Nin. She romanticized him in *The Diary of Anaïs Nin*, while he famously trashed her. I wanted to know why, so with my motivation spurred after his death on July 31, 2012, I sought access to Nin's archive. There, deeply immersed in Nin's handwritten pages, searching for clues, I found actual letters from Vidal to Nin and therein uncovered the truth.

Both Nin's diary and Vidal's memoir describe their initial meeting at a lecture in New York City at the end of 1945. She was an exotic creature with a lilting European accent, 42 years old, and still 20 years away from international fame. Vidal was the patrician grandson of a senator, about to become a published novelist, and only 20 years old. His memoir admits he might have "flirted" with Nin and states he went on to become "ensorcelled" by her. Her diary reports he asked for permission to visit that first night when he impressed her with his "manliness," "poise," and "greater worldliness."

Nin's diary entries suggest that six weeks after meeting, the two were behaving like jealous lovers. Vidal, Nin wrote, told her he was happiest with her and asked her to send away her husband, banker Hugh Guiler, so Vidal could have her all to himself. Their intense bond, according to Nin's raw diary, seems to have been colored by mutual attraction that was "undeniable, inescapable," but she wrote that because Vidal was homosexual, the pull between them could never be fulfilled. She encouraged him to undergo psychoanalysis. His response? According to her diary, he said, "Then I would become normal and take you away from Hugo."

Perhaps predictably, Nin's feelings of attraction for the young Vidal eventually cooled. She referred to their constant flirting as "the most painful of all relationships" and began pulling away. But the relationship was not cooling for Vidal who sent Nin increasingly anxious letters – letters that are included in her raw diary files.

Stunningly, Nin's diary reports Vidal began begging her to marry him, saying, "I built a house for us." But her emotional bond to Vidal had been irretrievably broken after she read her "portrait" in the manuscript of his third novel, *The City and the Pillar*. The novel tells the story of a young man named Jim who was obsessed by a homosexual encounter he had in high school. Jim develops a friendship with an older, exotic woman named Maria, but when they fail to fall into bed together Jim is convinced he is most definitely homosexual. Maria goes on to start an affair with another man and this makes Jim profoundly jealous.

Nin felt Vidal's portrait of her was a distorted caricature and this hurt her deeply. She wrote to him, saying:

I want to protect you the human being from the consequences of this incapacity to love, heighten, or transform, this sort of nausea about people, your poor opinion of them, for it will hurt you.

Nin then agonized about the relationship in the pages of her diary, marveling that she'd made friends with Vidal, but blaming the misunderstanding between them on her "romanticism," "sentimentalism," "great sadness," and "loneliness." She remembered Vidal had described his abandonment by his mother and she worried he'd been "crippled" because of it.

At this juncture the relationship was dead for Nin, but it was still burning for Vidal who scrambled to make extensive changes to his novel and assured her in a letter, "It is a very much better book now."

Then Nin met the actor Rupert Pole at a party in New York and they began a serious romance. According to her diary, Vidal's response was this:

> He puts on his glasses and acts like a senator, watching my love life ... with sad resignation, asking me to marry him, to bear his child by "artificial insemination." He says when no one else wants me he will still love me. ... And the other night during the party he repeated, "Marry me, marry me, marry me. I will lock you up in Guatemala ...."

Instead of joining Vidal in Guatemala, Nin embarked on a tour of the United States with Pole, thereby solidifying the relationship that would last the rest of her life. She evidently wrote a letter to Vidal from the road, a missive describing her "spiritual marriage" to Pole. By all appearances this letter devastated Vidal's hopes for a future with her, because at this point in my search I discovered concrete proof of his offers to Nin.

In a file for the year 1947, tucked in the diary's handwritten pages, is a remarkable letter from Vidal. In it, Vidal responded to Nin's news of her fulfillment with Pole by composing a letter of his own, one written on fragile stationery in his distinctive handwriting:

> Cherie
> Your sad Denver letter received and discounted. I was bitterly disappointed that you did not come down. You are quite necessary to me as you know. As for your fear that you would keep me from having a complete relationship, have no fear; I am quite alone here. ... I have adjusted myself to the fact that I shall never have a satisfying homosexual relationship. I am attracted to

youth, to beauty, and separately, unphysically, to you, to the spiritual emotional rapport we have had. I need that more than the other. I cannot, and this is strange, do without women. I like to think that it is not necessarily the mother in women that I want. ... I should like it if you can come down here and spend July or earlier whenever you're recovered. Now to speak of you. Are you trying to tell me (perhaps you have told me) that the Pole affair is everything you want and need? If that's so you should live with him. I wouldn't like it but I want you always to do, to be what you know, instinctively, is right. After all you have no real ties; Hugo is a shadow and I will accept it. Why don't you make this life for yourself? Surely the boy isn't a fool enough not to want to, to insist on having children, etc. ...

Cherie, here is my idea. I am offering the house for sale. If I can get 15,000, and I believe I can, I shall sell it. There is not enough stimulus in this place. I shall then go with you to Europe in January after *City and Pillar* is published. We can get a small place near Antibes or wherever there are interesting people and cheap living. I think we could do this very possibly. I want you to be independent and free of America, Hugo, all the mess. We can live there. Should I find a relationship, or should you, we would have to make some sort of adjustment but we have done that before and I am no longer worried. We can be tranquil if not complete. I must continue my search for boys and you must continue your slightly different one. But financially we can be fairly well off and independent. If I don't sell the house I shall lease it for 2 or more thousand and go anyway with you. If I get a Hollywood job then there will be a great deal of money. Think about this for I am serious. You must leave America or, if you stay, live with Pole.

Write me. I think of you as always.

Gore

Nin never accepted Vidal's offer of a sexless partnership and their once-vivid closeness dissolved into hostility: Gore Vidal's. Nin became bewildered by his growing resentment and her diary reports she asked him, "Why do you splatter venom on me?"

The reason was most likely his mother. Vidal had been abandoned by the woman when he was a boy and some believe her continued hurtful treatment of him further broke his heart. Anaïs Nin was a most glamorous replacement for a faithless mother: maternal, beautiful, infinitely interested – but doomed to repeat Vidal's abandonment for a second agonizing time.

Forty years later, nearly 20 years after Nin's death, Vidal wrote a memoir he called *Palimpsest*, a sizable portion of which was devoted to the assassination of her character. It accuses her of being a "chickenhawk" whose "hope" to have an affair with him turned into "a chagrin d'amour" that eventually became a "fureur," leaving the impression Nin had loved Vidal unrequitedly, was disappointed when he ultimately rejected her, and then was furious, bitter, and malicious. Vidal's chapter on Nin begins with this prevarication:

One of her biographers says that I, at twenty, proposed marriage to the lady, aged forty-three. She was, the biographer invents, to be my "front." Needless to say, I never wanted to marry anyone, certainly not someone who was to me, in my ageist youth, a very old woman.

Interestingly, a "palimpsest" is "a manuscript on which the original writing has been effaced to make room for later writing" – and perhaps this was a hint. Vidal turned his feelings for Nin neatly on their head, projecting his own sense of bitterness and bequeathing it to her. Why else would he have devoted an entire chapter of his memoir to a woman he had supposedly rejected?

Sifting through old letters in a basement room at UCLA, I discovered that Gore Vidal lied. It seems he loved Anaïs Nin deeply, so deeply he never got over her. His caustic wit masked his vulnerability and long after Nin's death he was still thinking of her, still writing of her, still stung by her inability to fill the void in his heart.

How on Earth Did She Juggle Two Husbands?

In April of 1949, while describing her activities in her private diary, Anaïs Nin wrote the incredible simile: "like a typical American wife."

Could it be true? Did this most exotic, most creative, and most rebellious of women actually live the life of a "typical wife" in that mid-century cul-de-sac of quintessential America?

I had stumbled across the description as I was examining Nin's unpublished journal entries and letters, pages she omitted from her famous published diary so as to protect those who loved her from her secrets.

The words "like a typical American wife" stuck with me for a number of reasons. Anaïs Nin had two raison d'etre, writing and love, and with both she refused to conform to the conventions of the day. In her writing, Nin found the usual "rules" so staid that she developed her own brand of storytelling in which she plumbed her characters' psychological depths somewhat in the fashion of a cubist painter. In a similar way, Nin's concept of love was anything but typical. She had cast off the usual wifely role 20 years earlier when, while living with her husband in Paris, she entered into an affair with a bohemian gadabout, Henry Miller, then layered in another affair with Spanish revolutionary Gonzalo Moré. In fact, when Nin wrote the words "like a typical American wife" she was awaiting word from a publisher on her novel *Four Chambered Heart*, the story of her relationship with Moré "without its sordid, degrading end."

But in a tellingly symbolic act, it was during this time Nin also telephoned an antiques dealer in hopes of selling

117

off the great symbols of her younger exotic and erotic life: her beautiful bed, lamp, mirror, and a coffee set. She explained:

> My attachment to them had died, and objects lose their glow as soon as we do not inhabit them, caress them. When they arrived from France after years in storage I saw they were dead – Antiques. Wreckage from great emotional journeys. ... They were objects I no longer loved – possessed only now of a discordant survival, which I am eager not to see again – eager to destroy.

Though it seems inconceivable such a woman would view herself as "typical," had Nin genuinely turned over a new leaf?

By the spring of 1949, Nin had solidified her relationship with Rupert Pole, her "second husband" with whom she was living in San Francisco. She described a normal day in which she was startled at 6:30 a.m. by the alarm clock and then began her morning routine: "I can wash my face and comb my hair and button on my slacks and sweater – and start the coffee and light the oven for the rolls." She and Rupert sat at the breakfast table with the *San Francisco Chronicle* and looked out the window to see men going to work and women waiting at the bus stop. And then:

> I drive him down the hill to the bus, like a typical American wife – We never talk very much – When I return I finish my coffee. I wash the dishes. Out of the windows of the kitchen I look down upon a wing of San Francisco, white houses on hills. ... I have become peacefully domestic ....

In reading these words, it would seem Nin had been absolutely tamed. But according to her diary, by late morning another reality pierced this marital idyll: "At eleven o'clock or 11:30 the mailman comes. It is a letter from Hugo, a very long one, describing his trip to Brazil."

"Hugo" was Hugh Guiler, Anaïs Nin's first (and only legal) husband, the man she had married in 1923. She had also been happily domestic in the early years of their marriage as seen in *The Early Diary of Anaïs Nin, Volume Three 1923–1927,* but it was Hugo who had later inspired her to construct an "edifice of lies" so as to pursue her much newer relationship with Rupert Pole. About Hugo, she explains, "I can't desert him altogether, and I can't leave Rupert."

At 46, Nin was firmly embedded in American life, deeply involved in the struggle to get her writing to the world at large, and regularly traversing the country to be with the two men in her life. I wondered how she was faring a few years into this arrangement. Was she still the "typical American wife"?

* * *

It is February 1953, the month Nin turns 50. Eisenhower is president. The average citizen has made way for that fabulous new "baby-sitter," the television. *Playboy* magazine features its first cover girl, Marilyn Monroe – who also had a hit with the film *Gentlemen Prefer Blondes.* And the average girl aspires to get married and have children. In short, the fashionably independent, capable, and exotic women of previous decades were subsumed in dreams of fulfillment via "home-making."

Nin, on the other hand, is still flying from husband to "husband," an early supporter of glamorous cross-country air travel. She is also deeply involved in psychoanalysis with Dr. Inge Bogner and is coming into a clearer understanding of why she is driven to live the way she does. And in the weeks before her fiftieth birthday, Nin has an operation in New York City to remove what turned out to be a tumor in her ovary. She describes the ordeal:

119

After 9 days I could go home. I wept with joy to be safe and sound again and at home. So grateful for Hugo. So grateful for the beauty of the house. ... Every day more strength. Horrors at the scar – feeling humiliated.

Hugo so kind – there, always there, when the truth is that he is weak, troubled, filled with fears, in need of help – I did not know until today how sick ... [Nin's ellipses] My illness restored him to his human self. ... Now it is the fear of failure (like Rupert!). But I did not realize how sick. My fears [about her health] were justified plentifully – but only now do I know how justified. He cannot bear to succeed – he cannot bear to fail. And this self-destruction of which I was unconsciously aware (as he must be unconsciously aware of my unfaithfulness) is there. Terrifying. The most difficult thing in the world to do is to admit, face, the weakness of the one from whom you seek protection! This is what I have had to do – And to help him.

So while Nin had sought refuge from Hugo in Rupert, she now finds similarities between the two men, similarities that frighten her.

In the midst of convalescing from her physical wound, Nin faces another painful reality:

I become more aware of the psychic illness once more: the fact I cannot face is that I am a failure as an artist. The publishers won't publish me, the book shops won't carry my books, the critics won't write about me, I am excluded from everything, neglected – and the very small, very small group of people who read me hide away carefully.

I cannot resign myself to this – because like Hugo, I cannot bear failure nor rejection.

Hugo had to pay for the publication of *Spy In House of Love* – he tried once more to protect me from the truth, poor Hugo ....

I don't understand either why I should care, lose sleep,

because Foshka of the Four Season Book Shop does not like my writing and refuses to sell my records – or because Wallace Fowlie writes a book on Surrealism and poetry and comments on the poetry in Miller and not a word on me – or because Kimon Friar "forgot" to come one evening. ...

We have so much to enjoy and we suffer from not being able to obtain what so many good artists failed to obtain – Kafka – Anna Kavan, Djuna Barnes – Isak Dinesen – Poor Hugo – both of us tormented by this need to win praise, love, understanding by our art – Why? Why? Why?

An interesting side note in this plaintive cry for recognition is that, while Hugo is the generous father figure from whom Nin seeks "protection," he has also finally fulfilled one of her early ideals in becoming a fellow struggling artist through experimental filmmaking.

On her fiftieth birthday on February 21, 1953, Nin is back in Los Angeles. Hugo writes:

Darling
It is a shame that your post office was closed Friday & Saturday so you did not get either the birthday telegram or letter I sent you. Here the P.O.'s were open Saturday.

I got your letter this morning sent Sunday & glad to know you are feeling the benefit of being in nature & the sun. Have no doubt you will always need that frequently & we will have to plan for it.

She must've had a short stay in New York, because on March 1 Nin was already on a plane heading back to Los Angeles. During the flight she wrote in her diary and, as was often the case, the passage is a long rumination on her relationship with Hugo:

The sun illumines what I write. I left a Hugo tender, forgiving, not angry anymore at my leaving, because this month, during my utter physical weakness which threw me completely under his wing, I was able to reverse the tides, and open myself to his needs, difficulties etc. with utter sympathy. Before this my guilt was so great that I could not allow myself to understand Hugo. When you have guilt all you can think of is that if you admit the guilt, the other one will again demand that you surrender. ... Guilt is self-censorship. To become free of it means to accept one's self as one is, and [the] reality of one's acts. To be free of guilt means one is free to understand [the] other's problems – I never had to give up what I could not give up by force – I had to accept myself, and therefore Hugo, and have sympathy for his difficulties.

One naturally wonders how Nin was able to continually leave Hugo without igniting his suspicions. And why did Nin have a need to leave in the first place? She writes:

Hugo feels a wife should be there all the time. When I leave he feels deserted. I feel the compulsion to leave, for many reasons – I cannot act otherwise at the moment. To admit my difficulties and recognize Hugo's, [illegible] the pain I cause him is what I was able to do for the first time. His many flaws, weaknesses, I once used as alibis for my leaving. I permitted myself an accumulation of irritations: he is clumsy, he forgets everything, he is chaotic, he is slow, he is unable to make decisions – and finally I had enough explosive to push off. But now I feel his flaws as human, pathetic. And I see mine too. I can bear to look at them. What Hugo is, I am fallible and defective in other ways – I am more volatile, more peripheral, I escape, I live split lives, I live by deception, roles, impersonations, duplicities. But in our distortions we are both "possessed." The effort we have made to put an end to distortions has been courageous.

As Nin comes to a new understanding of the dynamics of her psychology in relation to Hugo's, her unpublished diary reveals that she turns a corner in the marriage.

Hugo seems to understand the underpinnings of her motivations as well:

> I once saw Hugo in terms of what he had failed to be, in terms of my selfish, weak need of a father. Now I see him as like all the young sons I helped so well to gain strength on whom I lavished compassion and protection. ... I could not help him because I feared helping him meant surrendering my life as I must live it. But this is not what helping him meant. It meant understanding him. He felt my understanding, he felt that I was equally driven by forces outside of my desire, in the sense that they are shaped, patterned by the past and not by me today.
>
> For example: I look at myself with my own eyes. I evaluate them by my own set of values – But when it comes to looking at myself I looked at myself through my father's eyes. I judged myself by his standards, which I do not believe in. In his eyes I was not beautiful – I had flaws. All his standards were superficial, vainglorious, purely external.

As always, Nin's father rears his head. Freud theorized that we are forever marked by our first primary relationships in a kind of "family romance," forever slaves to those first beliefs, no matter how objectively incorrect. Naturally, one's partner would be a response to that primary relationship. Also, one's view of herself will reflect that primary dynamic. And as Nin illustrates, it might take a good 50 years to really understand that these unconscious "forces" have been at play all along.

As Nin comes to understand her relationship with Hugo more objectively, her raw, loose leaf diary discloses that she weighs him against Rupert and comes to a startling conclusion:

> Hugo decided while I lay unconscious on an operating table that our quarrels did not matter, that he did not want to lose me. I decided that in spite of his many

difficulties, he gave me a true love, big enough for me to trust as I never could trust Rupert.

For me this admission hits like bomb, because until this passage, Rupert Pole had been described as the "real" love, the true romance that brought Nin back to life.

Interestingly, 1953 was the year that marked Nin's sixth with Rupert. She had once memorably written that her relationships to Hugo and Henry both faltered at the six-year mark. This brings to mind the famous lore that a relationship loses its zing after a time, as memorialized in Marilyn Monroe's famous movie, *The Seven Year Itch*. Socio-anthropologists theorize that this is the period necessary for a man and woman to meet, produce a child, and raise that child to an age of relative independence – at which point the bond may weaken. Therefore, it appears the six or seven-year "itch" is not so much simple American comedy, but a hard-wired reproductive mechanism. For Nin, the six-year mark appears to have been the point at which she began to lose her ability to romanticize a man.

Still, Nin continues to approach her marriages in poetic terms and as a mystery, a dilemma arisen out of her unique psychology. She describes the trap in which she finds herself:

At each end an obstacle drives me away. At each end, I bruise myself against a fear, and run away. I do not leave of my own accord. I run away. The fears spring up barring the entrance at both ends: At Rupert's end, fears of jealousy, because Rupert is superficially attracted to many women, because the very nature of his neurosis motivates his flirtations. (Doubts of his power. ... He cannot make money and create a big life for a woman. Fear of the young girl he truly wants because she will laugh, or make demands, or expect too much, or treat him with the selfishness of young girls.) At Hugo's end other fears – or barriers. The Walls of China. The years I lived for and with Hugo alone were death for me. ... But it is no longer true.

Incredibly, as the years press on and Rupert loses his patina in Nin's eyes, she seems to re-embrace Hugo. She no longer uses the excuse that she can't "abandon" him. Instead, she realizes Hugo's value and importance in her life. At the same time Nin is obsessed with untangling the reasons she created her triangle marriages, she's hurt by the silence in response to her writing:

The other torment connected with NY is primarily concerned with achievement, activity, creation. The constant chess games of personalities are played in terms of this in the playgrounds of the season .... And so all my wounds are reopened. Kimon Friar says: "I have to earn a living at Circle in the Square readings, and so I have to have big names like Tennessee Williams, Lillian Hellman, Arthur Miller. I cannot afford not to have a full house." He may have heard that I did not have a full house last year when I read from *Spy In House of Love*. Just as Hugo feels deserted when I leave, and feels he needs me there continuously, I feel incurably rejected by the world at these manifestations that I have not won the place my work deserves.

But three months later, on June 9, Nin has a breakthrough:

Everything falls into place.
For the first time I am able to say to Hugo quietly, without deep disturbances, anger at myself, fear of his reaction etc.: I love my life with you, but I also need my life alone. This is the worst I have to tell you.
Hugo's answer was that it was better to be told this as a fact and not covered by excuses (lectures or trips etc.), which did make of each departure a shock. It is good that we admit it does cause him pain. He does not need a life alone. But he recognizes that I expressed this need

before we married, when I told him I did not want to be a wife, but a mistress. ... I accept wounding him because I also have made sacrifices for him: I sacrificed my artist way of life and my successful relationship to the world (for now it is clear that the abstract work was created to protect Hugo from the truth) ....

And so Nin counts the price of managing two marriages: her work suffers. In 1953, after years of writing, she is not able to present her undisguised work to the world, for it tells the story of her distinctly un-typical, un-American, and un-wifely life. She writes:

Everything falls into place: the absurd contradictions and splits in life and in work. I understand the relationship to the airy young men, the unreal, remote, non-human relationship to a distant father who was a volatile airy being ... the necessary relationship to deep, serious earthbound men (my reality). I understand my comfortable relationship to women (no danger. The mother having been the stable, fixed point of loyal love ...).

Hugo's fixities were necessary, his density and absence of volatility. All my irritations are gone. I accept myself (my own ideal of a wife prevented me from this, my own ideal of a woman) and Hugo (my need, unrecognized and against which I rebelled) but as [Dr.] Bogner pointed out, I myself had weights on my feet (weight of guilt) and I could never have lived the life I wanted: the weight was in myself, not the men.

Now I see everything clearly. I see distinctly that I want to be with Rupert but that [in] his life I reflect that I want to be with Hugo and that he may, in the end, turn out to be the greatest romance of all my life. If only I could recapture my original desire for him. Is such a thing possible?

Stunningly, at the six-year point it is Nin's relationship with Rupert that has become the trap, the bars of which are soldered in the sexual desire that has evaporated from her much-older bond with Hugo. She now laments her relationship to Rupert, writing:

> Desire will buy another airplane ticket, desire will pack a bag once more, desire will lead my steps into a life I detest, all of it, from the small deferences to manage, [such as the] rusty car, to a place and house I don't like, to mediocre friends who create nothing, to the sterility and emptiness of California. Rupert's body, face, passion able to create a moment of fire, a moment of altitude which is a trap and does not extend into the rest of our life together.

As the months pass, the relationship slowly sinks into the same morass that engulfed Nin's marriage to Hugo:

> I did not have this time the wild, frenzied desire to be with Rupert again. I feel he has slowly smothered the passion by seeking a wife and a domestic life while I sought to live with him only [in] the heightened moments of adventure. At the beginning I saw Rupert as a radiant, restless, mobile adventurer. I saw him climbing the highest peaks of Grand Canyon, and lying on his stomach so as to be able then to look over the very edge, while I stayed below, terrified and trembling – no fear of precipices.
>
> But today he is the young man full of anxiety about our not being married because it might be revealed to the Forest Service, and he is the young man who talks too much when people come for the special purpose to meet the writer Anaïs Nin, or who asks for homemade apple pie because it is better than the shop one, or who accepts passively the new government law that we must pay rent while actually [the] place belongs to government and strangers can use it like a railroad station. Garden is government property and requires special care (inspections now and then of home and

garden, for which we pay rent!). But – and this is what always disarms and castrates me, truly: Rupert cannot do better, and he cannot do better because his anxieties are too great when he attempts other professions. He chose the one he could most easily handle, and even then he suffers when he is asked to prepare a television program.

If I truly love Rupert, for his own sake I would see first of all that he gets analyzed – and then he would also be free of me, his passion, and realize I am not the wife for him.

Are Nin's disappointments with Rupert simply those that descend after a biologically-specified period of bonding? And is sexual attraction another kind of slavery, one from which we are eventually freed? Nin writes of her building frustrations:

Wednesday: Always when I arrive I am elated by the emotion of seeing Rupert and he is irritated by all the difficulties of meeting, misinformations by Air Line as to hour of arrival, last minute changes (too late or too early). Last night he had been notified that plane was arriving earlier so he had to rush – he arrived highly irritable. I always say: "don't spoil my homecoming!" He raves and rants at Air Lines. I say: "next time I won't let you come to airport – I'll just come home on my own." His pleasure has become anxiety – I was calmly waiting for him. He was afraid I would not wait etc. I don't understand all this, the tension and anxiety destroying the pleasure. Finally we are home. "You are looking mighty pretty – the leopard and white makes you look Russian."

In the dark, passion – recovery of the bodies, repossession of every part of the body – each one seeking bodies, both equally slender and nervous and electric. Rupert beside himself and after possession kissing my eyes and saying: "that is the only good thing about your going away, it is so good to have you again. Your return is so wonderful, so wonderful when you are back!"

If only I can keep my high mood, if only I can keep my altitude, even when our evening begins with Rupert killing a mouse with a broom, and eating synthetic Spanish rice (all ready to cook in cellophane) and a martini in a thermos tasting of tin cup. ...

I hold on to my precious Easter Egg of joyous expansion – not to lose it.

Rupert asks quietly for a mince meat pie. Tavi has been bathed in honor of my homecoming, but not brushed and he molts on me and on the rug. I paste the three novels together so that I can see what has to be done for the fourth symphonic movement. Rupert says: "isn't this so much better than an apartment in N.Y.? There is space, air, and quiet."

It seems that by spring of 1953, Hugo and Rupert have achieved a kind of equality for Nin. One is the "protector," the loving father with whom she can be "weak" and "selfish." The other man is "desire," the man with whom she can be sexual and romantic. She realizes she needs both men, and yet both drive her to distraction. In describing the striking similarities between them and the role she plays with them, Nin writes:

June 18 1953

When the two lives stand apart and opposite, I can balance them. It is when they weld by resemblances that I get lost. When I arrive in N.Y. I have to unclutter the apartment first of all, throw out the old magazines, the empty bottles, the worn out clothes, the discarded gadgets Hugo collects and then no longer uses. When I leave the apartment is alive, the objects have life. The mobiles work, the candlesticks have candles, etc.

When I return to Sierra Madre the same trash awaits me. Rupert never throws away anything. The broken plate he will someday repair (and never does), the torn old shirts, the Time Magazine, the house is cluttered.

I make it clearer and lighter, but Rupert impedes this activity and rescues useless objects out of the garbage cans! This haunts me and brings the two men into focus which distresses me, of father and son. ... Millicent [Nin's New York maid] says: don't give Mr. Hugo any more tables or shelves, he will only clutter them.

I have to give Rupert an explanation of why I threw away 10 year old fur boots so completely worn inside that they tear the skin of my feet or tear up whatever socks or stockings I wear!

A drama brought about by my request for a maid exhausts me and depressed me. Not again! I can't fight once more for independence, and the guilt attending my rebellions!

After reading the preceding passage, I must ask myself: are we doomed? Are we doomed to play out the ridiculous dramas dictated by our biology and psychology? After a long struggle for independence, is there no hope of personal freedom? After what for Nin was a 30-year battle to have her own voice and dictate her own life, was she not able to plant her merry flag and enjoy her life?

A breakthrough came in the life of Anaïs Nin after so mundane an event as this: at 50 years of age, she had made the decision to do the minimum of housework so as to pursue her writing. Is this, or something similar, not the auspicious moment for every married woman in America? Nin describes the outcome:

First of all I reorganized novels so that sequences and development of characters is infinitely clearer. By slashing and reshuffling scenes.

My mind is clearer than it has ever been. I feel sure, steady and integrated.

I worked on rearranging diaries – taking an inventory of all my work. If I do not write another word, I have produced a work to be proud of.

I feel coordinated, and about to solve my major problem.

But first of all order ...

I lie now on a chartreuse couch watching dinner. Rupert is watering the lawn. ... Rupert's passion is the same, but I am no longer jealous. I am detached, and I find myself free of jealousy, a marvelous victory. ...

But when you hold on to your own true character, people cannot interfere with your growth.

From the vantage point of middle age, in the midst of an All-American decade and not one but two primary relationships, Nin accepted responsibility for her life and her choices, gaining a new clarity as a result. The struggle and confusion of the previous decades was about to bear fruit in the forms she'd been craving: creative flowering, critical acceptance, and worldwide fame. She may have seemed anything but a "typical American wife," and yet Nin struggled with issues confronting many married women: She was compassionate and empathetic to her men, but also frustrated with their foibles. She sought to be protected, but was also the nurturing mother. She required some material support and craved sexual fulfillment, but found herself playing the role of unhappy maid. Finally, after years of agonizing, Nin restructured her life and gave precedence to her writing. Lo and behold, many problems fell away.

On the surface, a woman as exotic, creative, and rebellious as Anaïs Nin – a woman who wrote surrealist novels and published her diary and had two husbands simultaneously and broke taboos at every turn – would never be described as the "typical American wife." But under that surface, deep down in the subterranean realm where women struggle to find themselves, Nin was not so different from any of us. And so, once again, Nin called it. Anaïs Nin, in her way, was most certainly a "typical American wife."

The Day Anaïs Nin Became a Bigamist

Though Nin fell in love with Rupert Pole in the 1940s, she was still bound to Hugh Guiler, whom she'd married in 1923 when she was 20. Since she could not bring herself to divorce Guiler, she simply split her time between the two men and, incredibly, kept them a secret from one another.

I found the following entry enclosed in a box containing Nin's diary pages from 1955. This passage was written in March of that year after a lengthy description of her vacation with Rupert Pole in Acapulco, Mexico – a moment of "delight and euphoria." They had returned to Los Angeles in Pole's car and, on the long drive home, talk turned to his great wish:

Then on the way home he began to talk about marriage. It has been an obsession for seven years – first divorce and then marriage. I exhausted all the defenses I could invent. That I was neurotic, that I did not want marriage, that I wanted to stay as we were, that I wanted to protect him from a feeling of responsibility, etc. To no avail. I know the persistence of his obsessions. I also felt tired of resisting, feared the effect of my frustrating him, felt also an ironic mockery of the laws, a feeling that if this had to be a source of irritation and insecurity, oh well to hell with laws, I would gamble once more, one more gamble, I would grant Rupert his wish someday, and gamble on the consequences. It would relieve all the strain at this end.

But when Rupert stopped at Quartzsite, Arizona, before a Justice of the Peace, to inquire, and I let him, thinking there would be some obstacle or other (I don't have divorce papers!) he came out of the place radiant – his eyes blazing, laughing, his lips humid, his smile incandescent. "Let's get married!" He was at that moment irresistibly beautiful, so gentle, so happy, I felt like a murderer to kill his joy, yet I did it that time – but that did not discourage him. One week later we were driving to the place again and this time we went through the ceremony. I was moved. Rupert was sincere. The place could not be more isolated – a remote village [with] just a few houses, in the middle of the desert. A grey wooden house. An enormous, fat Germanic man, joyous, talkative. He had a beer-barrel stomach, a thick butcher neck. He could not be uglier, nor the place. Its ugliness was so extreme it became humorous. He had a joyous beer sincerity too. He read the words with dignity and simplicity. His name was Hardley. He wore, for us, a new fresh starched white shirt without a tie. He had on a small telephone table a huge book of Criminal Record. I smiled thinking the world will put my name down, but I knew that I was making one person happy in the present and that is a great and rare achievement. Rupert was happy, fulfilled, calm and grateful. He had been humiliated, harassed and worried by the situation. He pretended it was only legal protection, etc. but it was security – making peace with conventions.

I was elated by the danger, the adventure, the challenge, once more the overcoming of difficulties, the chess games with the world's literalness, and although my intelligence saw all the absurdities and danger of the marriage, emotionally I lived it with the utmost purity and wholeness, its deeper ritual, having felt deeply married to Rupert so many times – this was one more time.

Step Right Up:
The True-Life Story of Anaïs Nin's Amazing Life on the Trapeze

The soul is "a dark forest." So says D. H. Lawrence. And if the soul is a dark forest, a marriage of two souls must be an ocean, a secret language, a landscape full of creatures in its shadows.

What, then, would it be for a woman to be married to two men simultaneously?

Anaïs Nin believed the period covered in her diary starting in 1947 began "Part Two" of her life and required her to become a trapeze artist. When the story opens, she has been married for 24 years to Hugh Guiler. Nin had, at age 20 in 1923, done what was expected of all nice young women of the period and tied her star to a man, one to whom she was to give her unflagging loyalty in exchange for his economic support. She sincerely loved her "Hugo," but after six years living as a dutiful housewife, Nin realized the marriage could not be her all. She then entered into a long quest for more fulfilling love and in 1947 met the handsome Rupert Pole with whom a romantic relationship ensued. Nin discovered, though, she could not leave Hugo for Rupert. Thus, she began swinging from one man to the other on what was a particularly dangerous trapeze.

To better understand how Nin came to live this trapeze life, one must know something of her original wound, the psychic injury sustained when her composer father abandoned the family for a rich music student not much older than his daughter. After this shattering event, Nin's mother transplanted her and her brothers from their beloved Europe to what eleven-year-old Anaïs found to be the harsh reality of New York. She later said her father's desertion "crippled" her, causing her to lose her "confidence as a woman" and igniting within her an intense craving for love. But as is often the case, something else grew out of Nin's childhood amputation: an all-encompassing compulsion to turn her life into a gripping story within the private pages of her diary.

Nin's diary became her "refuge, home, shelter, jungle adventure," one that helped her "transfigure," as she put it, the "cruelties and abominations of human life" into the things she loved: art, poetry, and illusion. As Nin's locked closet filled with journals, she forged her own artistic path and ended up creating something quite innovative. Well before her time, Nin's work not only explored areas of human life both personal and universal, it also dissolved the false barriers between public and private, fiction and non-fiction, diary and novel, conscious and unconscious. She trail-blazed a style of writing that predicted the kind of communication we take for granted in our modern era. And by ultimately choosing to share huge swaths of her personal life, Nin foreshadowed our Internet Age with its seismic outburst of personal confession.

Of course it's easy to judge a dead woman who left a detailed record revealing her sex life. Deriding openly sexual women is one of society's favorite pastimes. As Nin wrote, everyone has an "original thought they don't want exposed for fear of ridicule," but she, through her diary and other writing, revealed not only her most original thoughts but also her most incendiary choices. As a result, her work has sometimes met with hostile misunderstanding and withering condemnation, yet in choosing to have her diaries published Nin knew very well she might be making herself a target.

Ironically, as a woman born a Spanish Catholic into a world still under the influence of the Victorian era,

Nin struggled alone with the complex issue of personal fulfillment. In what was an extremely bold experiment, she made the decision to live out her dreams and fantasies, and to describe the results in her diary. Ultimately, *Trapeze* illustrates the central reality that being a woman in the mid-20th century was – and perhaps continues to be – a complicated matter. It explores the problem of how to fulfill our boundless desires in the face of life's disappointments.

Nin's solution to her problems was to "split," and in regards to her relationships with Hugh Guiler and Rupert Pole this splitting provided the ultimate in comparison and contrast. As the trapeze act swung on and the epiphanies rained down, Nin began to understand herself. Gradually, she was forced to face the more elemental truths life offers us – that perhaps its limitations can't be healed by love, contained by moral attitudes, loosened by laws, or analyzed away by therapy. It turns out that arriving at happiness isn't so simple and, in the end, it was Anaïs Nin's marriage to her diary that saved her.

This secret diary, published for the first time, explores the problem of what it is to live with and be true to ourselves and to others while we are continually changing. It explores the conundrum of independence versus belonging, what it is to love and be loved, what it is to be family, and what it is to be free.

Here it is: The thrill. The spectacle. The danger. This is the hair-raising, fascinating, true-life story of Anaïs Nin's amazing life on the trapeze.

IN THE REAL WORLD
AT LATE MIDDLE AGE

Because she believed illusion protects us against painful events that might otherwise destroy us, Anaïs Nin tried to submerge herself in dreams. This strategy worked for many years, not only by making her life palatable, but also because it fueled the creation of her diary. Finally, though, at mid-life, reality hit.

I did extensive research on this period of Nin's life, both in her files held at UCLA and the papers stored in her home. I decided to zero in on unpublished diaries and letters from the 1950s and early '60s so as to understand how she fared during, what were for her, frustrating times.

The following essays reveal Nin's mindset as she struggled for recognition while finally confronting bleak facts of the real world, one that was often harsh and disappointing.

Can a Female Artist Survive the 1950s?

Is it possible to imagine a person as exotic, as European, and as experimental as Anaïs Nin living through the American 1950s, a decade of hamburgers and hotrods but also censorship and McCarthyism? This post-World War II period was one of deep conservatism, growing commercialism, and obsession with family that led to a "baby boom." It was a time when even Lucille Ball – one of America's treasures – was accused of being a "red." What did a daring iconoclast like Nin make of such a decade?

I knew that Nin had written and spoken of her unhappiness during the '50s, of the "silence" in response to her work, and of her dissatisfaction with the culture. But I also knew that during these years Nin was entering her own chronological fifties, a powerful and potentially difficult passage of change. What the materials I found revealed was that in the weeks immediately before she turned 51 in February of 1954, and continuing through the mid-'50s, Anaïs Nin struggled to find solid footing.

Perhaps symbolically, Nin wrote that she believed she was suffering from heart trouble. Another image she conjured was of punishment in a solitary cell. The lasting impression for me is of a prisoner serving out a time of confinement while the engine of her physical life and the seat of her feelings – her very heart – threatens to quit altogether. It is a vivid and painful image from a particularly difficult passage in a writer's life.

* * *

On February 10, 1954, after returning to husband Hugh Guiler in New York from another clandestine stay with Rupert Pole in mild Sierra Madre, California, Nin wrote this alarming description in her diary:

> When I arrived a month ago the plane landed in a snowstorm. It was 6am. I wore no rubbers. Several passengers shared a cold taxi which had difficulty in getting through the snow. All night I had felt such pain in the chest that I thought I would die of heart trouble in the plane. I was surprised to awaken alive. In the cold taxi I felt so weak I thought this was truly the end. Hugo had arrived a few hours before from Haiti. I got into a hot bath, to warm myself. In the bath my sense of illness and weakness overwhelmed me. I wept. I went to bed. I got up later to see Dr. Bogner. We arranged for a medical check up the next morning. It took all morning. No heart trouble, no tuberculosis, no cancer – but a low functioning of thyroid and lack of estrogen. I was given pills. The pain continued for a few days but the anxiety disappeared. Once more I was repaired by doctors.

Through this period, Nin repeatedly wrote of "heart trouble" associated with weakness. She had been told by a doctor that her heart would worsen with age and, upon telling Hugo this, he wept. Surely, Nin may have been suffering from physical illness or disease; she had undergone a grueling operation exactly one year before to have a tumor removed from her ovary. But Nin's life during the '50s was particularly stressful. Chief among her stressors was the fact that she regularly flew back and forth between two men and was compelled to keep the triangle relationship a secret. She felt forced to create elaborate stories to serve as excuses for the constant travel, and both the travel and the strain wore heavily. But there were other factors in her life that certainly affected Nin dramatically.

Nin's mid-1950s diary reveals that she suffered over

criticism, lack of understanding, and outright rejection of her writing. As I examined her papers stored at UCLA I came across letter after letter from publishers rejecting Nin's novels. While most were polite and genteel in tone, one publisher took another approach, stating with blunt finality that he found Nin's novels "pretentious." Later in the year Nin even wrote a letter to a reviewer in which she defended her work against what she felt was his total misunderstanding. And in the fall of 1954, Nin received a letter from a friend named Carol who wrote a long and detailed criticism of *Spy in the House of Love*, basically pronouncing it uneven. Nin responded with a letter of strong defense, explaining that the psychology of the character of Sabina is uneven and warned Carol not to "judge." Once again Carol responded, restating and underscoring her original criticism. Fascinatingly, this letter is ripped into pieces, but then taped back together. There was no continuing argument from Nin and no further correspondence from Carol.

Another source of stress was what Nin called her "failure" to succeed in supporting herself financially, in spite of her repeated efforts to do so through her writing. This pitched her into the hands of the two men in her life – men who, in her words, provided "protection" but who also made demands. On October 6, 1954, while in Sierra Madre, she wrote:

> The efforts I made this month to sell books, give lectures, were interpreted by Hugo as an effort to help him (by supporting myself) and to Rupert as an effort to earn my living here so I will not have to go to N.Y. too often. Both are true. And it is also true I failed. I earned exactly $100 this month!

Auspiciously, Nin then received a check for *Spy in the House of Love* from James Brown Associates for $186.62, along with note from "Joan," revealing:

I know you will be appalled at the size of this payment, but as far as we can tell the statement is correct, unless you have some different information. I hope that you will not decide to give up writing as a bad job.

To further complicate Nin's problems during this period, she experienced a deep distaste for American life. In November of 1954 she wrote:

It is true Rupert was raised here and can listen to the ugliest voices in the world discuss the price of the new Hilton Hotel, read Time Magazine – and accept mediocre people. But for the few moments of heightened life.

Later, she wrote:

Return to France impossible because it is a return to the artist life separated from the rest of the world – and possible only because of Hugo's work at the time. The concentration upon creation, which was my paradise: writing with Henry, and breathing the artist's life, is not possible here. Why? asked [Dr.] Bogner. I am not sure. I reconstructed for her the efforts I made to live with the artists here. I knew them all. But it was not the same. I remember when we tried to meet at the café on East 13th and Davis, the painter, turned on the radio to listen to a prize fight. It is intermittent, not continuous. And the fraternity is destroyed by competitiveness. The pressure from the outer world is greater. The pressure of economics, the problems of living. The atmosphere, the moral climate of Paris helped. Also absence of Puritanism and political pressure. I don't know what the artist life in Paris is like today.

Again, later, she continued ruminating on this issue:

So much takes place within me that by comparison I find a paucity, a stinginess, a silence in people which drives me to excess. I would at times be less of a rebel if people did not seem so inert, cautious. Am I creating my own isolation? It seems to me that most of my acts are of integrity. It is true I do not share with the many the cult of T. S. Elliot, or of Dylan Thomas. That I broke with "Living Theatre" after seeing play by Rexroth and Gertrude Stein. Sincerely, I do not care for the Sitwells. I do care about Tennessee Williams and Capote. Do I really deserve this Solitary Cell treatment?

To confound Nin's problems, she also experienced what are believed to be the classic signs of mid-life hormonal changes: waning energy, mood issues such as anger, and depression. Her self-awareness, as always, was vivid. In November of 1954 she wrote:

With Bogner I discover I cannot assume leadership, because of fear of my angers – of an uncontrollable anger that might explode. This anger is inextricably woven into my active and positive impulses. It forces me into passivity – a passivity I do not enjoy. Every active manifestation is followed by depression.

When Nin attended an exhibit of Henry Miller's watercolor paintings at the Brooklyn Library, she saw a publisher, someone she called, simply, "Laughlin" – a man who had, in Nin's opinion, been in a position to defend Miller's writing but who had not. She recorded the scene in her diary, once again framed by the growing intensity of her frustration:

When I saw Laughlin come in I said to myself: be careful of your hostility, Anaïs. ... I went up to him and said: "You made me so happy writing a letter in which you said my writing was deteriorating because for years I have felt your taste was deteriorating." He was startled but said: "Oh you must not take this personally!" I asked him during the meeting why he had not fought for Miller's books in court. He answered his lawyer had told him he could not win. But that is not a reason for not fighting, as we know from political battles.

Holding runaway horses of my angers!

She went on to explain:

I cannot bear to see myself as a person capable of anger – as one possessing a quick temper.
Repression of anger causes intensification of it.

Six months later, Nin described her continuing physical struggle and her exhaustion became apparent:

I haven't the energy to push it. The only thing of which I have become avaricious is my energy. I try not to waste it. ... What frightens me is that my energy is lessening – so I will soon accept, resign myself. The energy I have left I had hoped to use in getting out of America and finishing my major work.

My modern interpretation of this confluence is this: in her early fifties, Anaïs Nin was damned tired. She had struggled over 20 years for acceptance of her writing and, along with being ignored, fought criticism from publishers and friends alike. Because she had been unable to support herself financially, she felt trapped and was unable to escape or find a practical solution to her convoluted romantic relationships. As an added strike, Nin's inability to find in America a warm artists' community intensified her feelings of loneliness and her utter distaste for the art of this era added to her feelings of isolation. Finally, the symptoms of menopause, including her struggle not to reveal her anger just when it was coming to a roiling boil, only compounded Nin's dilemma. In the wake of all of these frustrations and heartbreaks, Nin was convinced she had "heart trouble" – and no wonder. This convergence of practical, creative, physical, and emotional issues threatened to defeat her altogether.

But Nin being Nin, she managed to pull herself together – at least on the surface. For example, in the weeks before she turned 51 and while working exhaustively to help Hugo present his experimental films publically, she wrote, "I managed, by dint of massages & facials to conceal the fatigue and to look beautiful." And after these "5 weeks of intense work (for Hugo)" she got on a plane to meet Rupert in Mexico. It was her intention to be well for him in every way and to bring about a repeat of past Mexican vacations. She wrote:

> But I had worked for it as the Thibetans worked to achieve their religious ecstasies. I had subjected myself to all the disciplines, analysis, doctor Jacobson and [Elizabeth] Arden – to emerge one morning at the icy airport all in ivory white wool, leopard belt and bag, festive, calm, strong, for life with Rupert.

To her delight, the vacation was a success and her pleasure with Rupert deepened.

After taking her restorative pleasures with Rupert in what was one of her favorite countries and in her favorite climate, Nin seemed to spend the winter of late 1954 and early 1955 preparing to ask herself whether she could continue the struggle to get her writing into the world. Then, shortly after her 52nd birthday, Nin realized she did indeed have the will to go on:

> Then yesterday I asked myself whether I had lost my power to create because of the many humiliations America inflicted on me, and the disastrous failure of the "Spy" – Am I beaten by the coldness, the stupidity of the critics, and the low level of the life in general? Has America's treatment of me triumphed?

She continued:

> The answer came this morning. The inner music started

145

again. I reread what I had done on Solar Bark and liked it. Tonight I hear the music, and all my feelings are awake.

And at this point she seemed to have greater insight into her process:

My greatest problem is one inherent in the experimental itself. Because I follow the pattern of free association, the design is sometimes chaotic even to me. The attempt to construct a novel in this way is difficult.

I wanted to show how the adventurer does not forget his past or escape it when he goes to the paradises.

And here is what is perhaps the most telling line:

Lillian [the central character who represents an aspect of Nin] does not escape – so she returns to remember and liquidate the past.

In the vast desert of Nin's mid-'50s America and after an arduous struggle for acceptance as a writer, she came upon a precipice and glanced over the edge into a terrible breach. What she saw she described after attending a musical presentation:

During the music, because the music was not good, I feel nevertheless reconciled to the idea of my personal death. It would be a pity if I died before completing my work, because I am an exceptionally fine instrument for human consciousness.

At the point of mid-life, through the lens of time, Nin seemed to have taken the long view and achieved a new wisdom. Though America in the 1950s had brought her to a kind of death, Nin then rediscovered her hunger to succeed. Indeed, she realized she was in the middle of what was a great life-struggle.

Fortunately, Nin had friends who were capable of delivering pep-talks just when she was ready to collapse.

Such was the case with Maxwell Geismar, an American author who sent flowers along with a letter to "Anaïs Pole" in what appears to have been late 1955. A portion of this letter reads:

> Dear Anaïs,
> What bothers me most in this whole thing is your conviction that you are 'through' as a writer, at least in this country, and that it is useless to go on writing; if that is what you really feel.
> This is death for a writer, and you must not accept this statement except as a momentary revulsion ....

In early 1956, Nin again struggled with her health. "This is the longest period I have had of low energy and depression," she wrote, "Two months, almost continuously gray." But by the middle of the year a fascinating document appears in Nin's diary files: a typed sheet upon which are handwritten the words "Pseudo Heart Trouble." Under this title is typed another title: "Symptoms." The sheet describes heart issues, pressure, palpitations, shortness of breath on damp days, and the fact that she had at one point exercised 15 minutes a day but by mid-1956 was only able to exercise five minutes due to "tightness" of her heart. The list continues:

> On an emotional level, I have been disturbed, but I am under analysis, for six years. Other illnesses: typhoid, anemia until the last few years chronic. Jaundice at 30. Stopped menstruating at forty-two. Have had hot flashes ever since with very little relief. Basically depressed, with temporary elations.

Nin's "Pseudo Heart Trouble" document is followed with a letter from a Dr. Harold Pardee in New York. Pardee's letter states that after administering tests he concluded Nin's heart was normal. A diary entry from Nin then states that "Bogner," her psychiatrist, suggested

Nin's heart issues could have been caused by anxiety and neurosis. Indeed, Nin lived for another 20 years and died, not of heart problems, but of cancer.

* * *

The image of the heartbroken writer serving out her time in a solitary prison cell is a chilling one. The 1950s were a painful, lonely, and frustrating time for Nin, but it is elevating to know that after laboring on for another decade, Nin transitioned out of this long and difficult phase, achieving breathtaking success as the writer of *The Diary of Anaïs Nin, Volume One 1931–1934*. This diary, written two decades before her darkest creative hour, catapulted her into the kind of fame and awarded her the sort of respect she'd always craved. Nin most certainly "liquidated" her past, shattering her solitary cell by making the very events that had haunted her entertaining and inspiring for others.

Nin, JFK, and Politics

It is no secret Anaïs Nin disliked politics. Her published diaries rarely describe the political events of her day and, instead, exist as a kind of walled garden of personal ruminations. For this apparent lack of awareness of the world outside, Nin has been criticized as a narcissist too self-absorbed to care about anything but her private life.

Take, for example, the period of the early 1960s. In *The Diary of Anaïs Nin, Volume Six 1955–1966*, no mention is made of John Kennedy's election in November of 1960. There is no report of the ominous construction of the Berlin Wall. Nowhere to be found is reference to the Cuban Missile Crisis in October of 1962. Finally, an event as appalling as Kennedy's assassination in November 1963 makes no mark on the pages of Nin's published diary.

Instead, jarringly, *The Diary* of the early '60s details Nin's interest in LSD. It includes musings on the pyramids and ponders "Gods [who] were angry at our invasion of the world." It tells the story of a girl's love for her pet raven. Finally, Nin's diary entry from the period of Kennedy's public murder tells a second-hand tale of a couple's sex life as influenced by the perfume of a jasmine bush that bloomed outside their bedroom window.

What can one make of the strange dissonance, the differential between the facts of the world outside and what seems to have been the interior of Anaïs Nin? Like a forensic detective I sought answers to this question in Nin's papers, dusting the premises for DNA evidence of the impact of one glaring political incident: JFK's assassination.

The first clue came as I examined documents on a

hot summer day in what was Nin's Japanese-inspired house, working through a cabinet full of her personal files. These cardboard files, labeled in the capital letters of her graceful handwriting, include clippings of articles, photographs, letters, flyers, speeches, and notes, and reveal Nin's interests to have been wide. A random cross section of file titles includes the following: "LAING" (for the psychiatrist R. D. Laing), "NEGRO REVOLUTION," "FEMINISM," "TAHITI," "LSD," "INTEGRATED CIRCUITS," "BALLET," "JAMES BALDWIN," "BALI," "FASHION GAME" (another file is labeled "DRESS"), "HAIR," "LILI BITA," "LOUVECIENNES," a thick file labeled "CANCER" (the disease that eventually took Nin's life), and, interestingly, "KENNEDY."

Nin's Kennedy file holds newspaper clippings of articles written in the aftermath of his murder. The first clipping is titled "Dallas Searches Its Conscience: The assassination of President Kennedy was the work of one individual. But a city now wonders if it should not take collective responsibility." The next article found in the pile is "No Theory Found Too Fantastic: Europeans Convinced Cabal Plotted in Dallas." The next article was written by the astute political reporter Walter Lippmann and is titled "Murder Most Foul"; it is accompanied by another article titled, "Endangering a Nation: Mosaic of Hate in U.S." Finally, Nin's Kennedy file concludes with an article from a French newspaper, entitled, "L'Evolution de le Politique Americaine."

Having established that Nin was indeed interested enough in Kennedy's assassination to keep a file of articles on the subject, it was time to move on to her papers stored at UCLA and work chronologically through those from the period of autumn '63. The first sign I came across relating to the assassination was a note from Nin's literary agent, Gunther Stuhlmann:

Dear Anaïs: Just a brief note – I am still under the shock of the Kenedy [sic] assassination which was just announced – to acknowledge contracts. ...

And then the flurry begins.

On the date of the assassination, November 22, Nin, who'd regularly flown from one coast to the other, was in Los Angeles with Rupert Pole. In 1963, Pole was her romantic partner of fifteen years and had supervised the building of the Silver Lake house they shared. Still, Nin carried on a frequent correspondence with Hugh Guiler, her husband of 40 years who lived in New York. A letter from Guiler to Nin dated November 23 contains no mention of JFK's murder, but immediately following is an undated letter from Nin to Guiler. It reads:

Darling:
I will call you today but this is just a note for your trip. Have been very upset about the death of Kennedy, as everyone has. Like a death in the family. He represented quality and intelligence and many other things. The ugliness is overwhelming. I believe it had a deep unconscious effect on America, perhaps first of all rousing their almost dead capacity to feel, then to become aware of their hostilities. And the dangers of it. All they can think of is to outlaw guns. But deeper thinkers are exposing the underlying hostility. And the worst of it is that many (I don't know what you think) feel it may not even be political, or psychotic, but pure money and oil well interests. That would be the final humiliation. Exposure of ruthless element. I would like to know what you felt and thought.

The file reveals that after Nin wrote the previous missive to Guiler she received a number of notes and letters from friends of the period, and all mention the assassination. These letters describe "three days of deep mourning" and "terrible days," and attempt to process in words what was obviously an event cited keenly on their collective emotional radar. Immediately after these communications from friends is Hugh Guiler's first recorded mention of the assassination, found in this letter to Nin:

NY.
Nov. 27, 1963

Darling,

... I enclose Walter Lippmann's article in case you did not see it and I had a talk with Bogner about something that this had stirred in me. There is of course something of a universal sense of guilt running through the whole country.

Two days later, on November 29th, Guiler wrote another letter to Nin:

I have been really shocked reading how the children (3rd & 6th grade) in many Dallas schools clapped and clapped when their teachers announced that Kennedy had been assassinated. The French and the [illegible] think there must be some plot behind the murder. They don't understand what you have been saying about the unconscious all along. Few want to look at themselves.

Continuing through the file, I found that within a nine-day period in December 1963 Nin wrote five letters to Guiler, four of which mention Kennedy's murder. They begin on December 3rd:

Darling: Received your first letter [as you were] en route to Paris. Your last day sounded harrowing, poor darling. ... It's funny I wrote you about similar assassinations in Paris and similar reactions (right blaming left, left blaming right) all the more striking as I went to see "Lord of the Flies." The reversion of children to barbarism very unconvincing in the story, based on finding themselves alone and having to hunt for food. Weak. As you say, not the real issue, which is hostility within.

Nin's next letter to Guiler is addressed to the Crillon Hotel in Paris and written on December 4th:

> Darling: So interested in your letter of Dec. 1 from Paris. Loved being able to visualize you in the Crillon. Loved description of Feux Follet, of reaction to Kennedy murder, clippings, your ideas on the subject. I'm afraid people are not ready to accept responsibility for hostility – all they are worrying about now is outlawing guns! And the worst crass I ever read was a report on cost of assassination! When I went for estrogen shot today Dr. said he had to treat hundreds of breakdowns.

As the days passed Nin's thoughts on the assassination seem to evolve, as gleaned from her December 6th letter to Hugo:

> Darling: Cristo Prohibito (Strande Decision) [sic] of Malaparte was all that we felt the first time.

Correctly spelled, *Cristo Proibito*, or *Strange Decision*, is an Italian film about a man who is determined to discover who was responsible for his brother's death. It was known in America as *The Forbidden Christ*. Nin's letter continues:

> It was sincere and deep, but once again, in the old tragedies (pre-Freud) the concept of the "innocent" is false. As we know now, we are all responsible in a deep way, for every hostile thought, and the saintliness of the mother, of the carpenter, is difficult to believe. It is strange that we have come back to the original sin, which is now awareness of our universal responsibility. I once felt innocent of the war, and therefore that I should not feel it (in London) but this innocence is really not true is it? Anyway, it was sad, noble, and I must say, I do owe America this feeling of collective guilt, for social and historical events.

And as Nin's letter continues, it's clear her preoccupation with Kennedy's tragic death had begun to give way to everyday life:

> Today work again. Yesterday took Piccolo [her dog] to have his teeth cleaned. He is a real ham. He acts as if it were a major operation, asked for a double ration of affection and food afterwards, looks as if he had come back from the dead etc. Really funny.

Then, in what appears to be her final letter to Guiler on the subject, Nin writes on December 12th:

> Darling: Pure poetry as we do is doomed. The tremendous union of America and Russia will give us 100 years at least of a prosaic, pragmatic, scientific, materialistic culture – representational art – etc. Even France! I feel the murder of Kennedy was symbolic, an omen – the murder of quality – of breeding etc. even if it was done by a psychotic – I think psychotics tune in on collective hostilities and act out the unconscious of the masses.

And here, references to Kennedy's assassination seem to end.

Clearly, the lack of political subject matter in *The Diary of Anaïs Nin* does not reflect disinterest by the woman herself. To the contrary, Nin was not only aware of the world outside her "walled garden," but her interpretations of at least one hideous event were sophisticated and insightful. Nonetheless, perceptions based on Nin's published diary have led critics to believe otherwise. As reported in *A Casebook on Anaïs Nin*, Nin was interviewed by Priscilla English in 1971. English asked the following:

> Certain members of the Women's Liberation movement have criticized you for spending so much time on your own self-development rather than directing your creative

energy primarily to political and sociological movements. How do you answer them?

Nin responded:

I used to have a sense of guilt about not being involved in the political movement. But recently I'm more and more convinced that none of the "systems" work except insofar as the quality of the people who practice within them is expressed. I think what is needed is a concentration on the quality of the individual so that the system can be raised by the caliber of the people working in it. The more work we do individually, the more enriching we can be to the group.

But Nin's distrust of politics in 1971 was not a recent development, for she had expressed these sentiments from her earliest diaries. In fact, the first line of a poem she had written at age thirteen was "Close your eyes to the ugly things," and this was a harbinger of strategies to come. The result is a published diary that seems a rarefied place, one that often locks out what Nin would call the "horrors" of the outside world.

Nin was a child of WWI and forced to abandon her beloved Paris at the outbreak of WWII, so it is not surprising she felt caught in an inescapable trap of capricious and "ugly" politics. She did not find answers in affairs of state or human systems, but, rather, in journeying inside into the world of dreams. For example, in Nin's *House of Incest*, a long prose poem published in 1936, she gives a strong clue as to her efforts to sidestep a painful "reality," but also where to find the truth behind the "lies":

To destroy reality, I will help you; it is I who will invent lies for you and with them we will traverse the world. But behind our lies I am dropping Ariadne's golden thread, for the greatest of all joys is to be able to retrace one's lies, to return to the source and sleep one night a year washed of all superstructures.

Nin's raw journal entries provide evidence that her lack of faith in politics was unwavering. In the fall of 1952 she wrote:

I find that I still hold the same disgust with politics, saying it is the biggest failure and mess ever created by man, the ruling of a world, that at least in art, the maddest, sickest, wildest, most useless artist could and often did achieve a moment of perfection. Where have we had a moment of perfection in the organization of community living?

And in another entry from September 8, 1953, Nin seemed cognizant of her appearance of indifference:

I am not blind to the horrors of the concentration camp. I only believe what I am doing is the creation of a world in which such cruelties could not take place.

But this seeming disavowal of politics must be balanced with Nin's actions in the "real world."

While examining files found in Nin's personal file cabinet, I discovered letters that had been written from and to her accountant, Roger Boulongne. A number of these letters attempted to sort out the complicated matter of Nin's legal residence, because the answer would determine whether Nin would pay taxes in New York or California. For me, what these letters provide is tangible evidence that Nin was a participant in civic life, because in a business letter of March 26, 1975, Boulogne wrote, "Your legal residence at present is New York City where you vote" and, in a note to Boulongne dated May 8, 1975, Nin wrote: "vote in N.Y."

The fact that political events rarely made an appearance

in her diaries, while in reality Nin wrote a number of letters describing her horror after the JFK assassination and (as the evidence seems to indicate) voted, supports – not the charge of Nin's narcissism – but Nin's penchant for compartmentalization. Nin's raw diaries from the period reveal that while living in Los Angeles with Rupert Pole, she objected strenuously to the intrusion of radio news reports, television (which she called "no vision"), and the presence of *Time Magazine* in their home. This intimates, not that one side ceased to exist, but that in attempting to protect herself, Nin split her life: the "ugly" facts of daily events versus the dream, the outside versus the inside.

What is especially enlightening about Nin's correspondence with Guiler regarding the JFK assassination is that it (and perhaps Guiler himself) was her receptacle and repository for her "real world." Meanwhile, Nin's edited diary became the "walled garden," the paradise of dreams that gave her respite from the horrors and viciousness of politics. Was lover Rupert Pole a part of this paradise, while husband Hugh Guiler was representative of the outside world?

What becomes obvious is that experience is something we curate for ourselves. Others may have criticized her choices, but Anaïs Nin was a woman as aware and opinionated about politics as any of us. She believed the reality of political events to be "ugly," so she worked to construct a new reality, one that sometimes existed only in refusing to acknowledge that which she couldn't abide.

On September 8, 1953, Nin wrote, "Beauty and poetry are selections we make from the chaos offered to us." Her published diary constitutes her selection.

Longing for Respect and Recognition

After 50 years of writing and in spite of gaining cult status, Nin had still not achieved the respect and recognition she longed for. I discovered the following unpublished letter while doing archival work in Nin's home. It serves as a testament to her struggle.

July 30, 1964

Mr. Howard B. Gotlieb
Special Collections.
Boston University Libraries.

Dear Mr. Gotlieb: I was away when your letter came. I appreciate your interest in my books and in my manuscripts. I wish we could talk about it, as it is a complex subject. Because I have not been a "commercial" writer, I am dependent on the sale of the manuscript of the diary (127 handwritten volumes, with photographs, letters etc.) as my only security for the future. The Library of Congress, Tulane University, Northwestern University and University of Southern Illinois, all have asked me for it as a gift. If, during the next few years there is any change in this (there may be when Henry Miller's letters to me appear in the winter, 430 pages, published by Putnam), and when I publish 500 pages of excerpts from the diary with one of the big publishers (not official yet) I may be able to make a gift, an idea which suits both my temperament and my dedication to writing and writers better than "selling."

Do you ever come to New York so that we may discuss this? I would like you to see the collection, and to ask you if you would be able to purchase it in the form of yearly payments like an income, or a professor's salary.

Thank you for your interest, and let us talk this delicate problem over some time.

Anaïs Nin

THE FINALE

In the mid-1960s, after an extraordinary life-long effort to not only fulfill her great craving for public acceptance but also to heal the wound that gave it birth, Nin found fame. Searching for clues about this important crossing in her life, I dove into unpublished material.

Here is the untold story of Nin's struggle for publication, as well as her reaction when it finally came.

Here, also, is a tremendously revealing private letter written near the end of her life – one not seen for decades. It exposes the true character of Anaïs Nin.

A Complicated Fame

After decades of writing, Anaïs Nin considered herself a failure.

It was the summer of 1965 and Nin was 62 years old. She had achieved underground status as a writer of surrealistic novels, yet she longed for greater acceptance, admitting it "mattered deeply" to her. She knew her best work was in her private diary, but not only was this document packed with dangerous secrets, it was also the emotional mast that kept her upright. Still, she wrote, "I must get the diary done before I die."

One of the reasons death was on Nin's mind was she'd had a number of surgeries. In fact, she'd experienced health problems all of her life and, late in 1965, was heading to the hospital for another operation. As she wrote in *The Diary of Anaïs Nin, Volume Six 1955–1966*, "I remember thinking that if I had not survived surgery I would have died believing myself a failure." Instead, when Nin awakened in her hospital room she was presented with the cover of what would be the first published volume of her diary.

I studied Nin's letters and unpublished diary entries from this period and found that a fascinating series of events took place, revealing both the professional and the emotional tests Nin underwent as she transitioned from private citizen to world-famous personality.

* * *

A letter stored at UCLA reveals that by 1964, things were moving for Anaïs Nin. On January 1st of that year, she wrote a note saying the following: "Editing Henry Miller Letters for Putnam's was a big job. Dating, connecting, finding sequence. Gunther is meticulous and works hard." Indeed, Nin's long journey to fame entered its last phase when *Henry Miller: Letters to Anaïs Nin* was published in 1965, because it made readers curious about the mysterious female recipient of his intimate correspondence.

Miller and Nin had what seemed an unlikely friendship in the 1930s after they met at her house near Paris. Miller was a coarse and nearly destitute ex-pat who expected only a decent lunch with a banker's wife, but when they discovered one another's writing, Nin and Miller realized they were wildly simpatico. The two unknown writers encouraged one another tirelessly and soon indulged in a secret romance. Partially through Nin's emotional and financial support, Miller achieved literary fame with the publishing of *Tropic of Cancer* (as well as a lot of trouble for flouting obscenity laws). Meanwhile, Nin remained relatively unknown, languishing in the mists of cult status.

The "Gunther" mentioned in Nin's note was Gunther Stuhlmann, Nin's literary agent who also edited the Miller letters and, in doing so, would ultimately stir curiosity about Nin. I found a letter typed on an official prison form. The writer was a pen pal of Nin's named Roger Bloom, an inmate in Missouri. He wrote that he was thrilled to read *Letters to Anaïs Nin* and was fascinated to "find so many comments of Henry's concerning you and your writing ...." Thus, with the publication of Miller's correspondence with Nin, an increasingly loud drumbeat was heard: Who was this Anaïs Nin? And what about her diary, the one that had been whispered about for decades?

But in spite of rising interest in Nin, she had reservations. I found this entry, dated January 1964, in her raw diary:

A strange world. ... Everything recorded, preserved. Yes, I understand later biographers will rummage through these treasures to immortalize and so and so. ... A strange world to those so occupied in living – unaware of documents. ... Frightening to see one's self or friends becoming history – what was personal and intimate made public.

Nevertheless, the files I examined also revealed that letters were flying back and forth between Nin and Alan Swallow, the independent publisher behind Swallow Press. A delicate black and white Japanese journal begun in September 1965 tells the tale, for in it Nin recounted that Stuhlmann and Swallow had come together in what became a joint effort to get Nin's diary published. A letter from Swallow dated February 23, 1964 confirms he had been sent the diaries: "Don't worry about the Diary. Anaïs, dear, I SO MUCH appreciate a chance to read this. ... [The] longing is great to be able to start the publishing of them."

However, as publication of her private chronicle became more than a dream, Nin's anxiety vaulted forward. I found this in the black and white diary:

[There] was a crisis. It began with a nightmare: I opened my front door and was struck by mortal radiation.

I grew fearful, anxious. I went to talk with [Dr.] Bogner. We discussed each fear separately. The main one was my concern with hurting others by my revelations.

Having written always with the conviction that no one would read it, I never censored myself. I wrote spontaneously. The fragments I showed were selected, as when I let Henry read his portrait and that of June because he was anxious about what I was writing – so there was frankness of the portraits.

There was another dream. My mother, no longer alive, was reading the diary and was as shocked as she was when I wrote a book about DH Lawrence.

There was another fear. As most critics had treated my novels so maliciously what would they do with the diary?

Bogner pointed out that most of my fears were related to past experiences. This taboo was my own.

The arduous task of finally getting the diary published was compounded by Nin's fear of making herself a target. As her black and white journal declares, "Suddenly it seemed to me I was exposing myself to the maliciousness of the world. No. I would not publish it."

But by fall of that year, Nin was forging ahead with efforts towards publication, though one of the great complications was her love life. A husband in New York City and another husband in Los Angeles did not know of one another and, miraculously, Nin had been able to sustain both relationships by living a bi-coastal life. For a number of reasons, publishing her journals presented dangers. For one, should her published diary reveal the existence of these men? A letter to her "first" husband partially answers this question:

Nov. 4, 1964

Darling [Hugo]: I was helping at the polls yesterday and so could not write you. I am a real community type now! But today I received your beautiful letter about the Diary. What struck me is not so much what you said at first but the wonderful way you said it. By gosh, you're turning out to be the writer of the family after all. After observing your artistry I settled down to enjoy what you said. It must be hard for you to read a story from which the principal character is absent, yourself. But someday the truth will come out. When you are rich enough to thumb your nose at the whole world.

Hugh Guiler's agreement to be left out of his wife's story is not surprising. In the 1920s, a young Nin was expected to disguise her real identity with a stage name when she danced in a public performance. Then again, after the financial crash in the late 1920s, Nin was discouraged from working because it would reflect poorly on her husband's banking career. Finally, Nin published her novels under her maiden name, Nin, rather than her married name, Guiler, and when Guiler began creating art he also invented an alias: Ian Hugo. Clearly, Nin and her husband lived in a time in which divisions and disguises of this nature were routine, and her husband apparently had no trouble – or Nin had little trouble convincing him – in being removed as a character in her diary.

But other difficulties were afoot. Publishers, many whom had leveled criticisms at Nin's "too personal," "too feminine," and "too European" writing, had long been her nemeses. Nin wrote this letter to Stuhlmann on November 5th:

Dear Gunther: Well, now that we are free of concern over the voting (I worked hard this time to get votes for Johnson) we can think about [Random House]. My intuition may be wrong, but I feel that in order to spare me, you are perhaps holding back some of the doubts of Silberman [an editor at Random House]. When I saw him my intuition was: When someone quibbles about little things it means they are not sure of the Big One. I did not feel he was sure, had faith, to carry it off. Let us see what happens after they read the last part. I feel in your last letter that you are beginning to sense all is not right. I try to put myself in their place, but I can't. For they would not have written the *Diary*. Please tell me what you know. Are they afraid? Do they miss the scandale, want the whole truth and nothing but the truth, is it too strong, too personal, unsalable?

Evidently, conversations had taken place between Stuhlmann and Nin in which it was decided her published diary would begin during the early 1930s, because this was when she'd chronicled her intense friendship with the now-famous Henry Miller. But beyond the artistic camaraderie,

Nin also had the secret romance with Miller and it seems Stuhlmann was aware of this fact. Nin decided to simply remove the sexual content from the diary and leave what remained, thereby protecting her privacy and Guiler's feelings. Still, Nin feared readers would intuit the secret "scandale" in the 30-year-old diary entries.

Stuhlmann responded to Nin's letter, explaining that in reading Nin's diary, Random House wanted sharp portraits of her friends who'd become famous, such as Miller, Otto Rank, and Rebecca West, but that they wanted less "personal" writing. They wanted "action" and "speed." Stuhlmann went on:

> I also have a feeling that Silberman may – perhaps subconsciously – be missing what you call the "scandale" although he has never said anything to the effect. ... I think his concern is still mostly about the impact the book will make when it comes out, to compete with the confessions of Simone de Beauvior et al. and one of his recurring themes is the thought that we "have to justify the expectations" which have been built up for so long. ... He is acting the editor, the businessminded publisher .... It shows us at least what we are up against. But don't worry, please.

And yet Stuhlmann's letter enflamed Nin's fear of criticism of her writing. She shot off this letter on the 9th:

> ... what they want would be destroying the integrity of the *Diary*. A diary is not an action film. What people. What greed, too, and entre nous, there is more in my diary than in the diary of Simone de Beauvoir. There is no action in hers, and no life at all. It is deadly dull. And all this talk about expectation. It shows lack of faith. No I feel, they are wrong.

On the 14th Nin wrote to Guiler:

... the attitude of [Random House] has upset me deeply. I admit that. I cannot understand it, and I do not want to discuss it with anyone, nor for anyone to know as I have had too much of that and most people have no faith. ... America tries to please the masses ....

To fuel her worries, Nin had yet another question: Would the person who was arguably the central character of her early '30s diary be willing to support its publication – or would he block her? On November 8, 1964 Henry Miller sent this note:

Dear Anaïs –
I'm almost sunk with work. Yes, OK on the release for "Diary." Suppose I ought to see proofs on "Letters" – don't trust that publisher!

And then, endearingly, this:

12/9/64

Dear Anaïs –
... The thing uppermost in my mind now is – don't you want to take out some, many, lines – short ones mostly – concerning our meetings, rendezvous, when are you coming, etc.? I ask because you always seemed so worried about revealing too much. Do you understand?

With Miller on board, the diary was a go. Swallow then wrote that, starting January 1, 1965, its publication would be his first concern. But on the 5th of January, Nin was forced to answer a panicked letter from her beloved cousin Eduardo. He had been an important supporting character in her diary, but he was afraid his sex life of the period might be revealed (he'd had homosexual relationships, which he considered "failed"). Nin responded by assuring him she did not "write to hurt" and suggested he take a pencil and cross out whatever he would not want published, or even change his name. In the end, though,

Eduardo was completely removed. Then on January 21st, Nin sent the diary manuscript to her brother Joaquin for his notes. His letters in return were extremely supportive and show an appreciation for his sister's talent. Nin's black and white diary described their exchange:

> Joaquin was tolerant and understanding, noting only the usual errors which arise in every family about the past. He reacted against my father's tendency to enhance and color his past. And I enjoyed legends and rumors which I never sought to confirm – Joaquin was cautious. "This was neither proved nor disproved." I the fiction writer opted for my father's embellishments. We reached a compromise.

It was a lot to absorb, as Nin's February 8th letter to Guiler makes clear:

> I am terribly disappointed that magazines have not taken the [Miller] letters, that Gunther does not keep me informed, that Putnam does not decide on the diary, that Bay won't do my next novel unless he gets Miller letters, no, of course, I do mind all that. But I am working. Next big hurdle is H. M. opinion of diary.

But, fortunately, that hurdle was well and truly scaled when Nin received a handwritten letter from Miller dated February 11th:

> Dear Anaïs –
> Writing (and reading) from bed. Now read about 200 pages. The stuff about June is dynamite. Aren't you worried she may sue for "libel and slander"? ... Am enjoying it immensely. Feel that you need to cut here and there because of repetitiousness. ...
> I think if publishers knew now what you have to offer they would descend on you in a swarm. Much of it truly sensational. You'll have to hide away once the book is out.

More later. Should be up & about by Sat. or Sunday.

Henry

[Postscript:] I wonder what June will make of it if she ever reads it? It's a Goya portrait. Would make me turn over in the grave. Funny, eh?

Miller then attached this gem:

Incidentally, you always seem to go places alone – question will arise – were you married, a widow or what?

Then, this note:

All in all, what impression I imagine reader will get – of you – is of a most complicated individual – and perhaps of a "solipsist" – one about whom the world revolves. No matter how clearly you analyze people and situations, one is left mystified.

Then:

It's an overpowering dose. There's a risk occasionally that your utter seriousness verges on the ridiculous. Watch for this – in editing. Repetitious phrases augment this danger.

And, finally, this communication from Miller is dated April 26th:

I don't think you should cut things (about me) that make me wince. Only what may be wrong or inaccurate. It isn't fair to the Diary to do otherwise. As for the others, I leave that to you. It's a difficult problem, I know.

Miller's magnanimity rings out from his letters and notes to Nin, and reignites a long-dormant friendship. In May, Nin sends Miller a letter in which she tells him she's read his comments and has removed things in her manuscript to which he objects. Nin and Miller appear to be reconnecting after a separation:

... it seems to me that the long lapse of time makes honesty less harmful, like a belated confession no longer part of human life, but the past. Thanks for the errors caught. They helped. As I told you before, I want the diary to do you justice, not injustice, even in small matters. Dear Henry, how do you think I felt the day I read in Fred's book* that I loved you abjectly? Please destroy this letter. I can't write you sincerely if I think of U.C.L.A. files.

(The irony of reading this private letter from Nin's UCLA file was not missed.)

And then *Henry Miller: Letters to Anaïs Nin* was finally out in the world. As Nin wrote to Guiler on May 3rd, "Reviews of Miller letters doing me good. Publicity, god of America." By May 31st, Swallow was zeroing in on Hiram Haydn, an editor at Harcourt, Brace & World, Inc. who claimed real interest in Nin's diary. At long last, Nin received a letter from Stuhlmann dated July 1st, 1965 saying Haydn was going to draw up contracts to publish the diary, that he and Swallow were going to have a co-production, and that the deadline for the diary manuscript would be October.

Unfortunately, in the midst of this long-awaited news, Nin was struck with new health issues. Doctors ordered her to stop the hormone treatments she'd been taking for some years and, as she wrote to Guiler, she experienced low energy, depression, and "mental disturbance." How could she face the gargantuan task of editing her diary? Nin recorded the moment in her black and white journal:

But another force, far stronger, was pushing me on. I had faith in the diary. I had put my most natural, most truthful writing in it. I was weary of secrecy, of showing only a small portion of my work. I felt the strongest and

---

* Alfred Perles' book, titled *My Friend Henry Miller: An Intimate Biography*, was published in 1956.

best of my work was there. I felt a maturity in the editing. I felt able to solve the problems. There was plenty enough to give so that what I could not give would not be missed. I could avoid the blank spaces. A driving faith urged me on. It was the vulnerable human being who trembled. But had I not always made these audacious leaps in spite of my fears? When I wrote the preface to Tropic of Cancer I risked losing everything, everyone who loved or protected me. It was an act of defiance and rebellion against the very world which sheltered me.

By July 7th Stuhlmann wrote telling Nin she'd made good cuts to her manuscript, bringing it down to 150,000 words, and this was still enough to be a "big book."

A continuing concern, though, was the former June Miller. She was Henry Miller's ex-wife and an intriguing major character of Nin's early-'30s diary, one who had fascinated a young Nin not only for her beauty and exoticism, but also for her lies. Their friendship had ended explosively in Paris 30 years previously when, upon finding that her husband and Nin were involved, June returned to America and had a breakdown. But during the run-up to the diary's publication, Henry Miller told Nin of one possible way to solve the June problem. He explained that June (who, amazingly, was working in an office as a typist) relied on friends named the Baxters. The husband, Jim, was a psychiatrist and he and his wife, Annette, had helped June achieve stability. Nin wrote to Annette, defending herself against June's accusation that she had been a treacherous friend. Instead, Nin wrote, she'd admired June and in publishing her diary from the early '30s would consider June's feelings. Nin explained her belief that if June hadn't made a "scene" and left Paris, she could've easily remained with the "passive" Henry Miller. After this initial correspondence with the Baxters, Nin then visited them and showed them portions of her manuscript that involved June. Nin told her diary, "They feel I was not unjust to her" and that she went on to forge a "sparkling" friendship with the couple. A letter from Annette states that after reading Nin's descriptions of the young June, Annette was amazed at how little June's essential character had changed in 30 years, but Annette also warned Nin that June would not like to be called a liar or even the use of the word "lies," a key part of Nin's portrait of June. Grafting on yet another secret in her life, Nin told her diary her friendship with the Baxters needed to remain unknown, because they were June's "refuge."

In the run-up to the diary's publication, Nin fielded a number of annoyances. For one, writer Rebecca West, a friend described in the early '30s diary, sent a telegram asking Nin to excise her from the manuscript. For another, Miller wrote telling her *Life* magazine had asked him to write a review the diary, but he had turned it down because it would be "too embarrassing," given his part in it, and he asks her to understand. He ends his note, exclaiming, "I'll pray for you!" But Nin's old nemesis, the *New York Times*, the "paper of record" whose reviewers had never liked her work, won the annoyance trophy when they asked her to write a review of D. H. Lawrence's plays and then re-wrote it, claiming her appraisal was "too feminine." Finally, in early November 1965 Nin had an operation to remove a gallstone. She later wrote it was "the usual nightmare – Fear of death, fear of anesthesia. Saying goodbye to the world from the window of the Doctors Hospital ...." But after returning home from surgery Nin received the proofs from the first volume of *The Diary of Anaïs Nin* from Harcourt. While savoring this victory, though, she also reached out to nutrition expert Adelle Davis for advice about her looming health problems.

It was the eve of the publication of Nin's diary. She had negotiated a minefield of potentially explosive issues, both professional and personal – and most too complicated for any one friend, family member, or business associate to understand. In March of 1966 she wrote this in her black and white diary:

One main theme emerged: I had to act according to my own nature or else the diary itself would be destroyed. ...

So, Dr. Bogner, the world appears as a vast jungle full of dangers to one's vulnerability. I have to venture not with a work of art, separate from myself, but with myself, my body, my voice, my thoughts, my feelings, expose them. ...

I felt the need to publish the Diary as strongly as the snake pushing out of its old skin, the crab desperately pushing out of his old shell grown too tight, too small. All evolution had this impulse. The impulse to give and the impulse to hide fought a mighty battle in this quiet office overlooking a garden. I would call it a battle between the woman and the creator. ...

After all, the fear of being judged is a very minor one. Every artist has taken that risk. She sits so calm, so serene, so wise. The small timorous concerns fall away. The main mature objective becomes clear. I believed every word I wrote. They were written by another self. So let this self, this creator, face the world.

At last, in April of 1966 the diary was published. Strangely, though, there is no celebration in Nin's personal papers, whether in the diaries still stored in her home or in the files held at UCLA. Instead, there's a ghostly chasm and one can almost feel the sense that Nin held her breath, waiting to see what the world would say about her life's work. Then there appears a short list of the writers of "wonderful, incredible reviews," most notably from the *New York Times*. And there's mention of an invitation to read her "Birth" story, for which she "did not have the courage." But at another media event,

They blew up photographs of Louveciennes for background. I read for half an hour. I read well but had impression they expected fireworks and I was restrained and quiet in my reading. Partly shyness. I saw B [Bogner].

Soon Nin was arguing with her publicity agent, a Mrs. Lindley, who decided to advertise Nin's new book in publications that had previously ignored or been critical of her, such as *Life*, *Time*, *Saturday Review*, *The New Yorker*, and *Partisan Review*. Also, Lindley would not advertise in *The Village Voice*, a newspaper that had given Nin positive reviews through the years. Lindley said, "I am trying to remove you from the underground where you were typed." Nin responded, "But I am part of the underground, I want to remain in contact with them. They supported me. The others tried to destroy my work." Once again, she found it necessary to visit Dr. Bogner.

The next month proved Nin's initial success was not just a dream. In a diary entry begun in May, Nin wrote:

A month of good reviews, love letters, appearances on television. Has the sniping really stopped?

Diary selling well. Hiram Haydn thought its sale would be limited. He only printed 3000. They were sold in a week.

A month which made up for every disappointment, every poison pen, for all the past obstacles. The sound of opening doors is deafening! Suddenly love, praise, flowers, invitations to lecture. ... The same publishers who turned down my work beg for my comments on new books they are publishing. ...

Book signing party at Cody's Book Shop, Berkeley. [Poet Lawrence] Ferlinghetti showers me with rose petals.

And in September of that year, Nin writes:

The past has not left any bitterness or revengefulness. I face the love, tributes I receive with pleasure. I am as if a new woman, born with publication of the diary. This new woman is at ease in the world because whatever shyness is left over from the past is helped by the fact that when I enter a room or a lecture hall people know me already and they rush toward me. The warmth creates a climate in which I can open, return the love, respond.

But long-awaited understanding and acceptance did not insulate Nin against practical problems. She was deeply disappointed when, after conducting numerous interviews with Oliver Evans, his biography of her displayed what she thought was a complete misunderstanding of her work. Meanwhile, she fielded requests for the gift of her original diaries to institutions such as The Library of Congress; she answered that "this was the only capital I had because recognition had come so late and royalties barely enough to live on." In September she wrote in her diary of the "problem" of people who "magnify the friendship I give beyond its genuine size. I hate to disappoint or hurt. I feel ungenerous not to be able to return in same amount, same temperature." And then, actual tragedy: On Thanksgiving Day 1966 her stalwart publisher, Alan Swallow, died at his desk of a heart attack. Sitting in Nin's living room, I read the many pages within her raw diary dedicated to her admiration for Swallow and her intense sorrow at his loss.

In spite of Swallow's death, though, Nin continued her work by plowing through the editing of *Volumes Two* and *Three* of her diary, readying them for what would be their eventual publication. Then in December she was in New York and taking care of Guiler, who was in Doctors Hospital being treated for his own health problems. She wrote in her diary:

For three weeks, up at seven, work on Diary last minute revisions, translate clockard, find spelling of language spoken by Inca who wrote Du Sang de la Volupte et de la Mort, translate merle blanc, how do you spell Dostoevsky.

Errands for Hugo. Telephone calls. Room 631. What do you need? Stamps. Ginger Beer. Envelopes. A file case. I arrive at Doctors Hospital after lunch, loaded. I sit down with my work if Hugo is asleep – or we talk.

The year of Nin's great splash of success with what had been her secret diary, something she'd created and labored over for more than five decades, ended in what seemed pedestrian fashion. She wrote that she'd "earned $9,500 – spent about $3,000. It is not enough to take care of Hugo." However, perhaps more importantly, she had not only earned "beautiful" reviews from the literary establishment that had previously seemed to reject her, but also, at long last, the recognition and respect of readers all over the world.

* * *

Over the next two years, Nin acclimated to a complicated fame. Her highly personal and "feminine" ethos was suddenly in vogue, and she became guru to thousands of readers, often young and female. To set the late 1960s scene, Nin noted in her raw diary a change in styles: "The girls wear high boots, skin tight pants, long hair, heavily made up eyes, false eyelashes, pale lips. The men wear boots, tight pants, wide belts, long hair." For some of these boot-wearers, Nin was not only their new favorite writer, but also a representative for their cause – a cause that was morphing as quickly as the seasons passed. Her life became one of interviews and speaking tours, writing assignments and preparation of future diaries, and hours spent filing in her Brooklyn vault or at home in Silver Lake.

Along with the newfound readership and adoration came attacks. A woman to whom Nin was introduced at a party said, "So you are Anaïs Nin. I hate women who tell all." Nin answered, "Perhaps because you have nothing to tell – or may not know how to tell it." And these demonstrations of hostility didn't always come from total strangers, for she was also fielding jealousy from more familiar sources. Startlingly, her Harcourt editor, Hiram Haydn, was a culprit. And in a letter to Guiler, Nin complained that, because she had gone from being "a failure" to being "successful," another close friend of theirs had suddenly become "petty." Clearly, the decades of criticism with their many slights and wounds still stung. For example, as she completed a glowing portrait of writer Leo Lerman for her published diary, Nin confessed in her raw journal that she still remembered the day in 1946 when her novel *Ladders to Fire* was published and Lerman had said, "Go and hide your head under a pillow." Over two decades later, Nin felt trepidation at the thought of seeing this man at a party. Her defense, as it had been since she was a teen, was a glamorous appearance: "I dressed up in my skirt from Singapore. I dress up to show my invulnerability, a pose in the world – to pretend I was not hurt."

Other relationships were rewarding. On January 27, 1968 Nin wrote about a lunch with her publicity woman, Hilda Lindley, during which they discussed the promotion of *Volume Two*. Nin felt they'd grown to have a wonderful "creative collaboration," though Lindley advised Nin not to expect as much "star billing" with the second published diary. No matter; the two brainstormed ways to attract attention to Nin's late-1930s diary, which described her purchase of a houseboat so as to live on the Seine river in Paris. "Let's have a party on a houseboat," suggested Nin and Lindley loved the idea. Nin told her raw diary, "She feels it is easy to work with me. I do not have prima donna's tantrums or exigencies ...."

Sadly, during this period Nin's health problems were

slowly gaining ground. Though a letter from a doctor dated March 22, 1968 declared that her pap smear had not detected cancer, something was amiss, for Nin's raw diary states: "Depression once cured by passion activity ecstasy – now permanent. No physical cause detected." "Passion activity ecstasy" had fueled Nin all of her life. Now, though she did not know it, she had less than nine years to live while facing the gargantuan task of getting her entire diary out into the world.

In the end, Nin did what she had always done, which was to turn to her original love, her diary. She wrote:

> I am out just to track down a figure, complete a story – pursue a denouement. I'm only excited when I find a clue, which leads me to a new facet or a new version of a story. I lie for the Diary.

*　*　*

Nin began writing her diary at age eleven in a state of heartbreak over the loss of her father. In it she spun the fairytale in which she cast herself as the beautifully-costumed heroine. It was also, she believed, the "lie" she told herself to make her life bearable, the "dream" that insulated her from the "deformities and homeliness," the "rust" of life.

Ultimately, Anaïs Nin's life was one of dedication, not to a man or a cause or a belief or a profession, but to the creation of a dream. Writing a diary made Nin's life bearable and, in doing so, out of thin air she created an astounding work of art.

Triumph Over the Original Wound

Anaïs Nin's diary began with a great defeat. Her father had left her for another young woman.

Nin felt the blow of that loss profoundly. It seemed a nightmarish amputation, one that filled her with fear, because – at least in her child's mind – it meant she was unlovable. It also, from an early age, established her apprehension about the role of wife. Therefore, even before she was married at 20, Nin realized she'd prefer what she perceived as the more powerful role of mistress.

Nin was born at the very beginning of the 20th century and came of age when women had vastly fewer opportunities. Abandonment, such as she'd experienced in childhood, was a real possibility, one that would leave her with very little legal or emotional recourse. Her solution, unusual though it may have been, was to secretly manage two marriages. In choosing this path Nin turned the tables and did what the Don Juans, the great male seducers such as her father, had done for eons.

By the time she'd achieved fame as a diarist in the 1960s, Hugh Guiler had been Nin's "East Coast husband" for over 40 years, while Rupert Pole had been her "West Coast husband" for 20 years. These men did not know of one another and Nin's diary reveals she sometimes suffered from terrible guilt about the arrangement, agonizing over the need to choose one man over the other, despairing that her self-made complications were unsolvable.

Clearly, Nin's childhood trauma held her in its grip, because she could not abandon as she had been abandoned, especially when she cared for both men. Guiler and Pole believed Nin spent time away from them for work and health reasons, but as fame and the possibility of exposure approached, Nin's love life became even more perilous and she needed to make painful choices. Finally, Nin was forced to face down her greatest fear.

Here is evidence of a great victory: Nin's very personal and private triumph, which I discovered as I read through her papers and diaries found in her writing room.

* * *

In a letter dated January 1964 and sent from New York City, Nin wrote to her "Darling" Rupert Pole with the usual excuses that she could not come "home" to their hillside house in Los Angeles. She explained that the University of Southern Illinois had shown interest in purchasing her diary. This possibility was important, because Nin was almost 61 years old and was – her words – a "failure." As a result, she was considering selling her diary (her "only capital") to the highest bidder. The truth was also, though, Nin had been in New York to take care of "East Coast husband" Hugh Guiler, who'd been hospitalized. On February 4th she wrote in her raw diary that she'd been with Guiler for ten days and "My Proustian work is my only joy, tracing webs and correlations."

What a difference a year made. Instead of merely hoping to sell her diary as a document suitable for dusty libraries, as 1965 dawned it appeared that portions of the gargantuan work might be published. In fact, Guiler had read parts and was supportive of Nin's efforts to publish it, but it had also been decided editing would include the total removal of him as a character.

Interestingly, in reading the copious letters exchanged by Nin and Guiler, there seems evidence for a great deal of affection between them. Guiler was a strong writer and expressed, not only interest in his wife's success, but enthusiastic support as well. But at this point Guiler was keeping abreast of the news by occasionally conferring with Nin's literary agent, Gunther Stuhlmann, and in a letter Guiler wrote to Nin on January 26, 1965, he exclaimed, "Gunther has told me he has now received the galleys approved by Miller. Congratulations! You did a fine diplomatic job there, which was why you went to L.A." Here it becomes clear from Guiler's letters that Nin most likely exaggerated her feelings of enmity for Henry Miller, no doubt to spare Guiler the dangerous revelation of Nin's and Miller's secret '30s romance. Also interesting is the fact that Guiler was sometimes reliant on Stuhlmann for information about her progress in publication of the diary. A long letter from Hugo dated July 3, 1965 ends with these sad words: "I do miss you and hope we don't have another long absence from each other. Love, H"

Nevertheless, as 1965 progressed and publication of the diary was assured, Nin began making moves to protect herself and protect her relationship with Pole. In a letter written by the publisher of *Henry Miller: Letters of Anaïs Nin* dated September 2, 1965, Nin is assured she's listed in their records as Anaïs Nin and not as Mrs. Guiler. Rather comically, the writer claims, "... we're not sure where that name came from." And then shortly before Nin's surgery in early November 1965, she wrote to a fiduciary representative, a Mr. Shively, to change her Trust to make Rupert Pole heir to her literary estate.

The Diary of Anaïs Nin, Volume One 1931–1934 was published in the spring of 1966 minus references to Guiler, in supposed respect for what she claimed were his wishes. Her published diary drew vivid, detailed portraits of her life in the early '30s, describing an intense friendship with Henry Miller and his wife June, as well as other relationships, but it failed to mention how and with whom she lived. Did she live alone? With family? Was she married? Had she been widowed? And how did she make a living? These questions proved troublesome down the line, but in the early days of Nin's fame, readers rode the dream of her fantastic adventures and didn't break the trance with practical questions.

Six months into her long-awaited success, Nin was in Los Angeles for the dawn of the new year. Over 50 years later, while sitting next to the fireplace in her purple living room in Los Angeles, I read through Nin's raw diaries of the period and found this entry:

> New Years 1967
> Rupert and I alone by the fire. A bottle of champagne. My handmade white wool rug I worked on in France, on which we lie and make orgiastic love.
>
> But I am not happy because Hugo is in the Doctors Hospital with a recurrence of his old hepatitis and I feel I should be there, but when I called the airline they answered there were no seats left.
>
> So I arrived in New York January 2 – went straight from the airplane to the hospital. Recurrence of hepatitis, recurrence of days spent in Doctors Hospital keeping Hugo company. Or being myself gravely ill. Hugo looks pale, but has no pain. It is a matter of rest, patience. He reads Laurents on Aggression.

Taking care of Guiler and making sure his needs were met had become a major concern for Nin. And then a year later, in January 1968, Nin's and Guiler's longtime maid, Millicent, broke the news she could no longer work. For the Guilers, it was "a very difficult break," because Millicent had been a member of the family and stepped in for Nin as caretaker during her many absences from Guiler. Nin and Guiler gave Millicent a pension and employed a new maid, a 63-year-old Russian named Verachka who, according to Nin's raw diary, is "straight out of Moscow Art Theatre." Nin explains in her diary that she found it necessary to see her psychiatrist, Dr. Bogner, because Guiler's health seemed to be slipping and "Hugo's illness always triggers off an attack of guilt." Then, on January 13th, Nin wrote in her diary:

Talk with Henry Westling, the rare book and manuscript collector. Talk on the Diary. If Hugo should stop working I will have to sell it. It is my only capital. In 1966 I earned $9,500 – spent about $3,000. It is not enough to take care of Hugo.

Because literary success and fame could not cure her old anxieties, Nin again made her way to her psychiatrist's office. Her raw diary reveals this:

I talked with Bogner. I cannot change or control my desperate irritation with Hugo – and I hate myself for it. Sunday Hugo and I took our familiar walk through the Village. Hugo's paleness worried me.

Though her sense of responsibility and horror of abandoning anyone would not allow it, Nin's diaries and letters reveal that her preference would have been to remain in Los Angeles with Pole. In fact she'd been quietly making moves away from Guiler and toward Pole, trying to ensure that Guiler would be taken care of, but also that Pole would be given his due as her true love. It was an incredibly uncomfortable position for Nin, but fame and age were pushing her there.

In a few months, however, the bomb Nin had always feared would hit her life. Though Nin and Guiler had, as far back as the 1920s, discussed the possibility of what we today would call an "open relationship" (and what they called "a whim"), the couple had once agreed to keep such a thing secret so as not to cause the other pain. Nin had adhered to this plan, though her intense relationships could hardly be called "whims." Pole, especially, had ruled her romantic life since the night she met him at a party in 1947. From that time forward, even when she was frustrated with him, he had become, at least in the pages of her diary, her "real" husband (and, in fact, they had indeed married in Arizona in 1955). And so when Pole guiltily confessed a minor dalliance, Nin angrily told him to keep his mouth shut, that she herself had her own secrets to tell. They then continued the devoted, passionate relationship Nin never achieved with Guiler.

And then the bomb exploded. By accident, a returned letter revealed that Pole had written to a lovely Japanese woman named Suzi whom both he and Nin had met in Japan during a vacation. Here's the raw entry from Nin's diary:

> Rupert's letter to Suzi discovered by accident April 20 1968.
>
> The anger – ideal behavior – generous and understanding. Sorrow. Is it the beginning of the end? The first fissure. He says no – no – minor – not major. Should I leave? No – He looked frightened. This happened two years ago! Last summer we went to Tahiti – I noticed no change. He could wait. I could not have waited, if I desired. He planned patiently. We would ask Suzi to accompany us. We would send a car – I would have been caught in the middle. In the letter to her he said: Anaïs cannot climb mountains – we will climb a mountain. But I who committed a thousand treacheries, how can I condemn? I who loved in dualities, triplicities, in fragments – of course I cannot judge – I will accept, encourage.

When Pole learned Nin had read his letter, he canceled his trip to see Suzi "without hesitation." But Nin wrote in her raw diary: "I will not use my power to destroy this small love. I will let it live." Nin then flew to New York, leaving Pole behind in Los Angeles claiming his love for her. But she continued in her diary:

Does he say it to persuade himself?
Repression
End of passion?
End of life for me.

After the talks, Rupert was passionate, clinging. Made love. I did not withdraw. A great victory over jealousy and fear to remain open and loving.

"You are not angry?" asked Bogner.

How can I be? She is lovely and intelligent and sensitive. He is sincere. He does not lie. We both fell in love with Japan and the Japanese woman.

It's a stunning achievement for the girl who'd been devastated by her father's desertion, who'd always feared abandonment, and who'd gone so far as to construct two homes so as to never find herself without shelter.

Nin then wrote this remarkable letter to Suzi, a copy of which I found in Nin's raw diary:

Dearest Suzi: This letter is a secret. It is written with love and understanding. By a freakish accident a letter to you was returned which I thought I had written and I opened it to add to it. It was R. writing to you. It was a love letter to you about seeing you in Japan. Because it was you, and I know your quality and loveliness, I could only be sad for the three of us. Because all of us are sacrificial and unselfish it is even more painful. I do not want you or R. deprived of anything. At the same time I cannot go to Japan knowing. I begged R. to go to Japan alone. It is important that nothing be denied or sacrificed. You know I believe that. I would never forgive myself for paining you or R. I would never feel worthy or even sure of his love again. Of course, now he says he will not go. He will sacrifice this to me. And I don't want such a sacrifice. If this is deep it must be lived out. I cannot even understand why R. did not plan to go last summer. But you Suzi are a woman, and women understand the needs of love. Please dear Suzi, treat me like a sister. I was concerned about the wistfulness of your face. Can you help me make a plan by which nothing will be sacrificed? R. will feel now he cannot go to Japan even if I plead with him, and promise to be there when he returns. But will you come? I would like you to come. I will help you come. I will be away. Both you and R. deserve whatever happiness may come of this. You can stay at Bernard Forrest house. He will be in Japan. You can see R. I will find things to do. I say this with love and trust and only ask you not to tell R. Then at least we will know if it is a relationship more important than all others. I have lived by the rules of love alone and so I feel others should live too. You do understand how guilty I would feel if this were ignored, and how this might estrange me from R. far more than knowing I had been, accidentally, instrumental to its destruction of something alive. Write to me at another address 4255 West 5th Street Los Angeles 90005. I will be in New York for lectures May 3 so unless you answer me immediately then after that write me care of Gunther Stuhlmann 65 Irving Place, New York City 3. He is my agent. If we do not go to Japan we can invite you here. Do you have a vacation? We were not even sure if you had any leisure. Do you teach all summer? As you probably know, R's school ends June 20 or so. I can be away at any time you can come. Can you come? I will keep this secret from R. It will be our secret. If you tell me you want to come, I will send you a ticket. You can stay as long as you want to as long as you can. I have lectures up to June 12. But there are many things I can do to be far away. I can go to Europe. If this is impossible, will you meet us in Europe, in Paris? I can also find ways to disappear. I want to be the cause of your happiness not your unhappiness. R. asked me where I wanted to go this summer. I can say any place but Japan, if you cannot come. I always dreamed that if R. had to love another woman it might be someone like you.

For years, Nin labored in the pages of her diary to know herself, to understand her hunger for connection. *The Diary of Anaïs Nin* was created out of a great longing, as is all art. But when she discovered that Rupert Pole (arguably her true love) secretly schemed to romance another woman, thereby potentially replaying the abandonment Nin had experienced as a child, Nin was truly put to the test.

Nin's letter to Suzi makes clear that after being held hostage by a childhood defeat (the very experience that had given birth to the diary), she had finally escaped her jailer and slipped the trap. Anaïs Nin's philosophy, for good or for bad, for better or for worse, is crystalized in this line written in her letter: "It is important that nothing be denied or sacrificed." In writing the letter to Suzi, she demonstrated she was willing to extend to others the love, the understanding, and the freedom she had sought all her life.

Anaïs Nin privately created her ultimate ending, one of triumph over her original wound.

THE FUTURE

Nin always sought connection – with her true self and with the true selves of others. She (who adored Parisian café life with its hours of shared intimacies) longed for a "café in space," which is a perfect metaphor for the Internet and social media. Nin would love that this new technology allows us to keep in contact, tell our stories, explore new ideas.

Anaïs Nin's diary is especially relevant today and we're ready to view it through a new lens. In the following essays, I project into the future as to the significance of her incredible life-long record of consciousness.

The Diary as Myth-Making

The creation of a self through diary writing was, for Nin, an act of survival. Writing was the way in which she could gather her "emotionally splintered" life.[*] And because her obsessive journaling was an attempt to remain whole through a tenuous narcissism in the wake of shattering events, Nin's diary became, according to one critic, a "claustral shrine of self-consciousness."[†] But isn't this true of all art? Isn't all art an act of will, an effort to impose order on the chaos of experience, an expression of the self, an effort to reveal something of that self to oneself and others?

The pages of a diary cannot contain the true self in any real sense, but a self that is an interpretation, an arrangement of facts and fictions, a construction. A diary can only reveal the echoes and reverberations of a self. As Nin wrote in the second volume of her published diary, the process of "selecting details to create a persona" is for the most part unconscious, so that the blank pages of a journal seem to become a kind of "mirror before which the diarist stands assuming this posture or that."

Diary writing is a myth-making procedure, a potent dialogue with aspects of the self, one in which the diarist documents and contains her process of being. Nin believed she was able to capture the essence of her real personhood

---

[*] Nin, Anaïs and Henry Miller. *A Literate Passion: Letters of Anaïs Nin and Henry Miller 1932–1953*. New York: Harcourt, Brace and Jovanovich, 1987.

[†] Mellow, James R. Review of *A Literate Passion: Letters of Anaïs Nin and Henry Miller 1932–1953*. *New York Times Book Review*. 17 January 1988.

in the pages of her diary. Rather than recording what she saw as the banalities of living or the events taking place in the world, Nin believed her task was to journey inward and discover a self.

The quest for a self cannot, ultimately, be resolved, because the nature of the self, just like the nature of reality or the nature of truth, lends itself to myriad interpretations and cannot be resolved. We do, though, leave a trail of clues, fingerprints so to speak, that give evidence to our having once been here.

Anaïs Nin's Relevance for the 21st Century

Anaïs Nin was not entirely understood or appreciated during her time and, until recently, it's been easy to dismiss her work and life.

Why? First, Nin was a female writer who did not have a formal education, but who kept a diary about her interior life. Strike one, two, three, and four. But to add to what was considered the triviality of Nin's work, much of it focused on her private experience, exploring feelings about relationships. Then, it turned out that in exploring her feelings about relationships, Nin conducted a great experiment in violating taboos. She left religion as a teenager. She cheated on her husband. Then she cheated on the man with whom she was cheating on her husband. Then she had a brief affair with her father. She conducted a passionate affair with a black man. She took the virginity of a seventeen-year-old. Then she had two husbands. Add in an abortion. And I swear to you, reader, these are not the most interesting facts about Anaïs Nin's life.

Nin recorded her private feelings and experiences in her diary, and then made this diary public. It may be difficult for younger people of the 21st century, who regularly indulge in what is in essence public diary-keeping, to understand what a brave act it was for Nin to publish her diary. In doing so, she was adhering to her own values, yes, but she was also exposing herself to social and professional crucifixion. How many of us could be that brave?

I believe it's taken the invention of the Internet to understand Nin's work. It's brought a new blast of understanding of consciousness, for good and for bad. We seem to now better appreciate the "stream" of our experience, the fact that it is ongoing from birth to death and can be expressed and shared in fragments. The advent of social media – which Nin would have deemed a "café in space" – brings a new way of knowing others, of what we today would call knowing their "truth."

Nin somehow understood this stream of our consciousness and the importance of personal truth, and she created a record of her life that hits a universal vein. In the 21st century, Nin's diary hurdles the old judgments of being too personal (as opposed to "appropriately" public), too feminine (rather than "correctly" masculine), too self-centered (rather than "acceptably" outer-directed), too edited and fictionalized (as contrasted to the strictly "factual"). Her diary jumps these now old-fashioned barriers. These judgments built walls, walls that separated and separate us from understanding one another, but these walls are now liquidating – then reassembling – then liquidating again before our eyes.

The day might come when, instead of clinging to our disparate poles, to our walls and judgments, we realize that our momentary fragmentation of experience eventually melts into one big consciousness. To understand one person is to understand something of yourself. To have empathy for yourself (because you've been saddled with this self without your permission), you may eventually understand and have empathy for others.

How can we know ourselves or know others? Through story. As long as we humans exist on earth in this form, our need to tell stories – to ourselves and to others – will never die. Stories give order and meaning to our lives and evidence of our consciousness.

Anaïs Nin was just a heartbroken Spanish girl who kept a diary of her most private thoughts and feelings, and one day her diary will be appreciated as one of the most significant stories of the 20th century.

BIBLIOGRAPHY

Anaïs Nin Papers, c. 1910–1977. UCLA Library, University of California at Los Angeles, Department of Special Collections.

Bair, Deirdre. "The Making of *Anaïs Nin: A Biography*: Paul Herron Interviews Deirdre Bair." *A Café in Space: The Anaïs Nin Literary Journal.* Volume 7. 2010.

Casillo, Charles. *Marilyn Monroe: The Private Life of a Public Icon.* New York: St Martin's Press, 2018.

Churchwell, Sarah. *The Many Lives of Marilyn Monroe.* New York: Metropolitan, 2004.

Field, Joanna. *On Not Being Able to Paint.* Los Angeles: J. P. Tarcher, Inc., 1957.

Friedan, Betty. *The Feminine Mystique.* New York: Dell, 1964.

Hall, Calvin S. and Vernon J. Nordby. *A Primer of Jungian Psychology.* New York: Mentor, 1973.

Heck, Micaela. "Under the Skin." *Psychology Today.* October 2017.

Kakutani, Michiko. "Nin's Diary Reveals Troubled Life, Mind: Writer Shown as Highly Self-Absorbed." Review of *Incest: The Unexpurgated Diary of Anaïs Nin 1932–1934*, by Anaïs Nin. *New York Times Book Review.* 4 December 1992.

Lawson, Nigella. "Adventures of a Superfluous Woman." Review of *Anaïs Nin: A Biography*, by Deirdre Bair. *New York Times Book Review.* 11 May 1995.

Mellow, James R. "Review of *A Literate Passion: Letters of Anaïs Nin and Henry Miller, 1932–1953*, ed. Gunther Stuhlmann." *New York Times Book Review.* 17 January 1988.

Nin, Anaïs. *The Diary of Anaïs Nin, Volume One 1931–1934.* New York: The Swallow Press and Harcourt, Brace and Jovanovich, 1966.

—— *The Diary of Anaïs Nin, Volume Two 1934–1939*. New York: The Swallow Press and Harcourt, Brace and Jovanovich, 1967.

—— *The Diary of Anaïs Nin, Volume Six 1955–1966*. New York: Harvest/HBJ, 1976.

—— *The Early Diary of Anaïs Nin, Volume Three 1923–1927*. New York: Harcourt Brace Jovanovich, 1983.

—— *The Early Diary of Anaïs Nin, Volume Four 1927–1931*. New York: Harcourt Brace Jovanovich, 1985.

—— *Fire: The Previously Unpublished, Unexpurgated Diary 1934–1937*. New York: Harcourt Brace & Company, 1995.

—— *Henry and June: From the Unexpurgated Diary of Anaïs Nin*. New York: Harcourt Brace Jovanovich, 1986.

—— *House of Incest*. Ohio: Swallow Press, Ohio University Press, 1958.

—— *In Favor of the Sensitive Man and Other Essays*. New York: Harcourt Brace Jovanovich, 1976.

—— *Incest: The Previously Unpublished, Unexpurgated Diary 1932–1934*. New York: Harcourt Brace Jovanovich, 1992.

—— *Linotte: The Early Diary of Anaïs Nin 1914–1920*. New York: Harcourt Brace Jovanovich, 1978.

—— *Mirages: The Unexpurgated Diary of Anaïs Nin 1939–1947*. Ohio: Swallow Press/Ohio University Press, 2013.

—— *Nearer the Moon: From A Journal of Love: The Unexpurgated Diary of Anaïs Nin 1937–1939*. New York: Harcourt Brace & Company, 1996.

—— *Trapeze: The Unexpurgated Diary of Anaïs Nin 1947–1955*. Ohio: Swallow Press/Ohio University Press, 2016.

—— "The Writer and the Symbols." *Two Cities: The Revue Bilinque de Paris*, 5. 1969.

Nin, Anaïs and Henry Miller. *A Literate Passion: Letters of Anaïs Nin and Henry Miller 1932–1953*. New York: Harcourt Brace Jovanovich, 1987.

Pierpont, Claudia Roth. "Sex, Lies, and Thirty-five Thousand Pages." *The New Yorker*. 1 March 1993.

Vidal, Gore. *Palimpsest: A Memoir*. New York: Penguin Books, 1996.

Made in the
USA
Middletown, DE